职通中文
Access to Vocational Chinese

急救护理（基里巴斯版）

Emergency Nursing (Kiribati's Edition)

郁云峰 总主编
于天琪 谭方正 龙杰 副总主编
聊城职业技术学院 编

初级篇
Elementary

中国教育出版传媒集团
高等教育出版社·北京

图书在版编目（CIP）数据

职通中文. 急救护理：基里巴斯版. 初级篇 / 郁云峰总主编；于天琪，谭方正，龙杰副总主编；聊城职业技术学院编. -- 北京：高等教育出版社，2025.3.
ISBN 978-7-04-064057-1

Ⅰ．H195.4

中国国家版本馆 CIP 数据核字第 2025FE0427 号

ZHITONG ZHONGWEN JIJIU HULI (JILIBASIBAN) CHUJIPIAN

| 策划编辑 | 李 玮 | 责任编辑 | 杨 漾 | 封面设计 | 张 楠 | 版式设计 | 张丽南 |
| 责任校对 | 蔡 丹 | 责任印制 | 赵 佳 | | | | |

出版发行	高等教育出版社	咨询电话	400-810-0598
社　　址	北京市西城区德外大街 4 号	网　　址	http://www.hep.edu.cn
邮政编码	100120		http://www.hep.com.cn
印　　刷	北京中科印刷有限公司	网上订购	http://www.hepmall.com.cn
			http://www.hepmall.com
			http://www.hepmall.cn
开　　本	787mm×1092mm 1/16		
印　　张	19.5	版　　次	2025 年 3 月第 1 版
字　　数	316 千字	印　　次	2025 年 3 月第 1 次印刷
购书热线	010-58581118	定　　价	108.00 元

本书如有缺页、倒页、脱页等质量问题，请到所购图书销售部门联系调换
版权所有　侵权必究
物　料　号　64057-00

编写委员会

总 主 编：郁云峰

副总主编：于天琪　谭方正　龙　杰

主　　编：孙志强　戴　波

副 主 编：夏一雪　王　慧　李玉涵　李正大　田红燕　綦旭良

编辑委员会

主　　　　任：肖　琼　孙云鹏

项目负责人：李　玮　盛梦晗

项 目 编 辑：李欣欣　杨　漾　陆姗娜　蔡　丹　熊世钰

专家委员会（按音序排列）

陈曼倩	哈尔滨职业技术大学	崔永华	北京语言大学
梁赤民	中国-赞比亚职业技术学院	梁　宇	北京语言大学
刘建国	哈尔滨职业技术大学	宋继华	北京师范大学
宋　凯	有色金属工业人才中心	苏英霞	北京语言大学
赵丽霞	有色金属工业人才中心		

前　言

为进一步推动各国学习者中文语言能力和专业技能深度融合，提升学习者围绕特定行业场景、典型工作任务使用中文进行沟通和交流的能力，持续满足中文学习者的职业规划和个人发展需求，实现优质教育资源共享，促进多彩文明交流互鉴，教育部中外语言交流合作中心联合有色金属工业人才中心，根据各国"中文+职业技能"教学发展实际需求，以中国职业院校为依托，组织职业教育、国际中文教育、出版和相关企业等领域的专家，共同研发"职通中文"系列教材及配套教学资源。

"职通中文"系列教材参照《国际中文教育中文水平等级标准》和《职业中文能力等级标准》，分为初、中、高三个等级。各等级均遵循"语言和技能相融合""好学、好教、好用"的编写理念，依据相关职业的典型工作场景、工作任务和高频用语，设计课文、会话、语言点和练习等板块，不断提升学习者在职业技术领域的中文应用水平和关键技术能力，为学习者尽快熟悉和适应工作环境提供帮助。本系列教材适用于在中国企业从事相关专业的各国员工，同样适用于在华留学生或长短期培训人员，也适用于有意向了解中国语言文化和职业技能的学习者。

《职通中文　急救护理（基里巴斯版）　初级篇》是"职通中文"系列教材之一，适用于在医疗卫生机构急救护理岗位的员工。通过学习本教材，学习者能够用中文进行简单的工作交流，了解急救护理的全流程操作技巧，读懂中文岗位说明书。

教材对标中国国家卫生健康委员会发布的《需要紧急救治的急危重伤病标准及诊疗规范》《护理分级标准》等行业标准，由护理行业专家把关，根据医疗机构对从业人员的总体要求，将实际工作场景和典型工作任务中的真实语料，重构成适用于"零基础"学习者水平的课文和对话。全书共30课，每课包括复习、热身、生词、课文、语法、汉字、拓展和小结等八个部分，同时配有丰富的图片，力求以图文并茂的形式呈现真实的职业场景，此外还配套开发了音频、视频等资源，帮助学习者掌握在职业场景中用中文进行基本交际的能力。

学习者学习本教材后应当可以：

1. 具备基本的中文理解和运用能力，为职场应用和中文进阶学习打下基础；
2. 掌握护理工作中常用的基本词汇、专业术语及常用表达，并应用到日常交际及工作岗位中；
3. 对中国文化具有基本的理解和认识，能够注意到与中国客户沟通交流时的文化差异，提升职业竞争力。

本书得到了教育部中外语言交流合作中心、有色金属工业人才中心和专家组的支持，我们在此表示衷心感谢。本书还得益于聊城职业技术学院和高等教育出版社的鼎力支持和精心指导，在此一并致谢。

"职通中文"系列教材的出版和应用能够促进各国"中文＋职业技能"人才的培养，推动当地经济发展，从而为构建人类命运共同体做出积极贡献。由于项目团队学识和相关经验有限，加之时间紧迫，许多疏漏、不足有待完善。恳请本书的使用者将发现的问题反馈给我们，以便再版和编写相关教材时改进。

本书编写组
2024 年 11 月

Preface

In order to further promote the deep integration of Chinese language proficiency and professional skills among learners from various countries and enhance their ability to communicate and interact in Chinese in specific industry scenarios and typical work tasks, the Center for Language Education and Cooperation under the Ministry of Education, in collaboration with China Nonferrous Metal Industry Talent Center, has organized experts from vocational education, international Chinese education, publishing, and related enterprises to jointly develop the "Access to Vocational Chinese" series of textbooks and supporting teaching resources. Based on the actual needs of "Chinese + Vocational Skills" teaching development in various countries and relying on Chinese vocational colleges, the series aims to continuously meet the career planning and personal development needs of Chinese learners, realize the sharing of high-quality educational resources, and promote exchanges and mutual learning among diverse civilizations.

In reference to the *Chinese Proficiency Grading Standards for International Chinese Language Education* and the *Chinese Proficiency Standards for Vocational Education*, the "Access to Vocational Chinese" series of textbooks is divided into three levels: elementary, intermediate, and advanced. All levels follow the writing philosophy of "integrating language and skills" and "being easy to learn, teach, and use." The textbooks are designed around typical work scenarios, work tasks, and high-frequency terms of relevant professions, with sections on texts, conversations, language points, and exercises, continuously improving learners' Chinese application skills and key technical abilities in the vocational and technical fields, providing assistance for learners to quickly familiarize themselves with and adapt to the work environment. This series of textbooks is suitable for international employees engaged in relevant professions in Chinese companies, international students or trainees in China, as well as learners interested in Chinese language, culture, and vocational skills.

Emergency Nursing (Kiribati's Edition) (Elementary) is one of the "Access to Vocational Chinese" series, which is suitable for employees engaged in emergency care in medical and health institutions. Through learning this textbook, learners can carry out simple work communication in Chinese, understand the operational skills of the whole process of emergency nursing, and read the Chinese job description.

The compilation of the textbook was based on industry standards such as *Urgent Treatment of Critical Injuries and Illness Standards and Diagnosis and Treatment Norms* and *Nursing Grading Standards* released by the National Health Commission of China. Industry experts were hired, and the requirements of medical facilities were surveyed. The actual work scenarios and authentic language in typical work tasks were combined to re-constitute the text and dialogue in line with the level of beginners. The textbook consists of 30 lessons, each of which includes eight sections: review, warm-up, new vocabulary, text, grammar, writing, extension, and summary. It is richly illustrated with pictures to present real work scenarios in a visually engaging manner. In addition, audio, video and other resources have been developed to help learners acquire the ability to perform basic communication in Chinese within vocational contexts.

After studying this textbook, learners should be able to:

1. Develop basic ability to understand and use Chinese, laying a foundation for workplace application and advanced Chinese learning;
2. Master basic vocabulary, technical terms, and common expressions used in nursing work, and apply them to daily communication and work exchanges;
3. Gain a basic knowledge of Chinese culture, recognize cultural differences when communicating with Chinese clients, and improve professional competitiveness.

This book has received great support from the Center for Language Education and Cooperation under the Ministry of Education, China Nonferrous Metal Industry Talent Center, and the expert panel, for which we would like to express our sincere gratitude. We also extend our thanks to Liaocheng Vocational College and Higher

Preface

Education Press for their strong support and guidance.

The publication and application of the "Access to Vocational Chinese" series of textbooks aim to develop talents with "Chinese + Vocational Skills" across the globe, promote local economies, and make positive contributions to building a community with a shared future. Due to the limited knowledge and relevant experience of the project team, coupled with the time constraint, there are certainly many omissions and shortcomings that need to be improved in this book. Users of this book are kindly requested to give us feedback on the problems they find so that we can improve them when republishing and compiling relevant teaching materials.

Compiling team,
November 2024

目 录 Contents

第一单元
UNIT 1

院前急救 Pre-hospital First Aid	1
第 1 课　认识急救 Lesson 1　Understanding First Aid	2
第 2 课　快速评估 Lesson 2　Rapid Assessment	10
第 3 课　病情分类 Lesson 3　Disease Condition Classification	19
第 4 课　摆好体位 Lesson 4　Positioning	28
第 5 课　急救要点 Lesson 5　Key Points of First Aid	37

第二单元
UNIT 2

急诊分诊 Emergency Triage	47
第 6 课　急诊科 Lesson 6　Emergency Department	48
第 7 课　分诊方法 Lesson 7　Triage Method	57
第 8 课　收集信息 Lesson 8　Collecting Information	67
第 9 课　初级评估 Lesson 9　Primary Assessment	77
第 10 课　次级评估（问诊） Lesson 10　Secondary Assessment (Consultation)	86
第 11 课　次级评估（生命体征） Lesson 11　Secondary Assessment (Vital Signs)	96

VI

第 12 课	次级评估（身体部位）	106
Lesson 12	Secondary Assessment (Body Parts)	
第 13 课	测量体温、脉搏和呼吸	116
Lesson 13	Measuring Body Temperature, Pulse, and Respiration	
第 14 课	测量血压	126
Lesson 14	Measuring Blood Pressure	
第 15 课	测量血氧饱和度	136
Lesson 15	Measuring Blood Oxygen Saturation	
第 16 课	紧急救护	146
Lesson 16	Emergency Care	

第三单元 UNIT 3　外伤救护技术　Trauma Rescue Techniques　157

第 17 课	外伤止血	158
Lesson 17	Trauma Hemostasis	
第 18 课	止血带止血	168
Lesson 18	Hemostasis with Tourniquet	
第 19 课	外伤包扎	178
Lesson 19	Trauma Dressing	
第 20 课	四肢绷带包扎	188
Lesson 20	Limb Bandaging	
第 21 课	手部绷带包扎	197
Lesson 21	Hand Bandaging	
第 22 课	膝部绷带包扎	206
Lesson 22	Knee Bandaging	
第 23 课	踝部绷带包扎	216
Lesson 23	Ankle Bandaging	

第 24 课 Lesson 24	三角巾悬吊包扎 Triangle Bandage Suspension	226
第 25 课 Lesson 25	骨折固定 Bone Fixation	236
第 26 课 Lesson 26	前臂骨折处理 Forearm Fixation	247
第 27 课 Lesson 27	小腿骨折处理 Lower Leg Fixation	257
第 28 课 Lesson 28	搬运伤员 Handling the Injured	267
第 29 课 Lesson 29	双人搬运 Two-man Handling	277
第 30 课 Lesson 30	多人搬运 Multi-people Handling	287

Unit 1 第一单元

院前急救
Yuànqián jíjiù

Pre-hospital First Aid

第1课 Lesson 1

认识急救
Rènshi jíjiù
Understanding First Aid

热身 Warming Up

看图选词。Look at the pictures and choose the correct words.

A 护士 (hùshi) nurse   B 医生 (yīshēng) doctor
C 病人 (bìngrén) patient   D 急救 (jíjiù) first aid

1   2    3    4

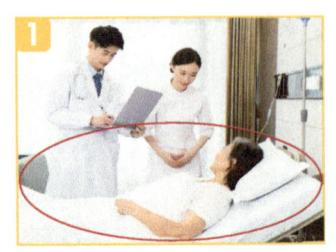

学习生词 Words and Expressions 🎧 1-1

| 1 | 认识 | rènshi | v. | know |

2

第1课 | 认识急救

2	院前	yuànqián	n.	pre-hospital
3	急救	jíjiù	v.	first aid
4	是	shì	v.	be
5	名	míng	measure word	(used for people)
6	护士	hùshi	n.	nurse
7	医生	yīshēng	n.	doctor
8	学习	xuéxí	v.	learn
9	护理	hùlǐ	v.	nurse
10	急危重症	jí-wēi-zhòngzhèng	n.	critical illness
11	病人	bìngrén	n.	patient
12	要	yào	v.	should/must
13	尽快	jǐnkuài	adv.	as soon as possible
14	抢救	qiǎngjiù	v.	rescue
15	救护车	jiùhùchē	n.	ambulance
16	赶到	gǎndào	v.	arrive
17	家里	jiālǐ	n.	home

3

词语练习 Words Exercises

1. 看图说词。 Look at the pictures and say the words.

2. 词语分类。 Categorize the words.

A 护士　　　B 急救　　　C 医生　　　D 抢救
E 病人　　　F 赶到　　　G 救护车　　H 护理

1 名词（nouns）：_____
2 动词（verbs）：_____

学习课文　Text　🎧 2-2

Rènshi　jíjiù
认识急救

Wǒ shì yì míng hùshi, Wáng Tiān shì yì míng yīshēng. Wǒ xuéxí
我是一名护士，王天是一名医生。我学习

jíjiù hé hùlǐ. Jí-wēi-zhòngzhèng bìngrén yào jǐnkuài qiǎngjiù.
急救和护理。急危重症病人要尽快抢救。

第 1 课 | 认识急救

Jiùhùchē, yīshēng, hùshi yào jǐnkuài gǎndào bìngrén jiāli.
救护车、医生、护士要尽快赶到病人家里。

Understanding First Aid

I am a nurse, and Wang Tian is a doctor. I study first aid and nursing. Critically ill patients should be rescued as soon as possible. The ambulance, doctors, and nurses should arrive at the patient's home as soon as possible.

课文练习 Text Exercises

1. 判断正误。True or false.

1. 我是医生。
2. 王天是护士。
3. 急危重症病人要尽快抢救。
4. 医生、护士要尽快赶到病人家里。

2. 选词填空。Fill in the blanks with the correct words.

A 急救	B 急危重症	C 病人家里	D 医生

1. 王天是_____。
2. 院前_____很重要（hěn zhòngyào，very important）。
3. 救护车要尽快赶到_____。
4. _____病人要尽快抢救。

5

学习语法 Grammar

语法点 1　Grammar Point 1

特殊句型：" 是 " 字句　Special sentence pattern: the 是-sentence

由 " 是 " 作谓语构成的句子，主要表示肯定、判断，即说明事物等于什么或者属于什么。常用结构：A ＋是＋ B。否定形式：A ＋不（bù, not）＋是＋ B。
The sentence composed of "是" as the predicate mainly expresses affirmation and judgment, which explains what something is equal to or belongs to. The common structure is: A ＋是＋ B. The negative form is: A ＋不＋是＋ B.

例句：
1. Wǒ shì hùshi.
   我是护士。I am a nurse.
2. Wǒ bú shì yīshēng.
   我不是医生。I am not a doctor.
3. Zhè shì jiùhùchē.
   这（this）是救护车。This is an ambulance.

语法练习 1　Grammar Exercise 1

按照正确的语序连词成句。Make sentences in correct orders with the given words or phrases.

1. ①护士　②我　③是
   _____

2. ①医生　②是　③王天
   _____

3. ①我　②医生　③不是
   _____

4 ①是 ②这 ③急危重症病人

语法点 2 Grammar Point 2

能愿动词：要　Modal verb: 要

能愿动词"要"表示情理上必须这样，后接动词。否定形式：不用（yòng, need）。

The modal verb "要" indicates that something must or should be done, followed by a verb. The negative form is: 不用.

例句：

1 医生、护士要尽快抢救病人。The doctors and nurses must rescue patients as soon as possible.

2 救护车要尽快赶到病人家里。The ambulance should arrive at the patient's home as soon as possible.

3 医生要尽快赶到。The doctor needs to arrive as soon as possible.

语法练习 2 Grammar Exercise 2

把"要"放在句中合适的位置。Put "要" in the right place in the sentence.

1 医生____尽快____赶到。

2 护士____抢救____病人。

3 救护车____尽快____赶到____病人____家里。

4 我们____抢救____急危重症____病人。

汉字书写 Writing Chinese Characters

yī 一

èr 二

sān 三

sì 四

文化拓展 Culture Insight

Chinese Language

Chinese language is the most widely used language in China and also the language with the largest number of first language users in the world. It is one of the six working languages of the United Nations and one of the official languages of the World Tourism Organization. Mandarin is the standard language of modern Chinese, with Beijing dialect as the standard pronunciation, northern dialect as the basic dialect, and exemplary modern vernacular texts as grammatical norms. Mandarin is the national language of China. Chinese characters (ideograms) are written characters that record Chinese language and are commonly used in China.

第 1 课 | 认识急救

小结 Summary

词语 Words

朗读词语。Read the words aloud.

| 医生 | 护士 | 急救 |
| 救护车 | 抢救 | 急危重症 |

语法 Grammar

朗读句子。Read the words aloud.

1. 我是一名护士。
2. 王天是一名医生。
3. 急危重症病人要尽快抢救。
4. 救护车要尽快赶到病人家里。

课文理解 Text Comprehension

根据课文内容选词填空。Fill in the blanks with correct words according to the text.

A 尽快　　B 救护车　　C 病人家里　　D 急危重症

_____病人要_____抢救，_____、医生、护士要尽快赶到_____。

9

第2课 Lesson 2

Kuàisù pínggū
快速评估
Rapid Assessment

复习 Revision

朗读词语。Read the words aloud.

| 医生 | 护士 | 病人 |
| 急危重症 | 院前急救 | 抢救病人 |

热身 Warming Up

看图选词。Look at the pictures and choose the correct words.

A 循环 (xúnhuán) circulate   B 快速 (kuàisù) rapid
C 气道 (qìdào) airway   D 呼吸 (hūxī) breathe

第 2 课 | 快速评估

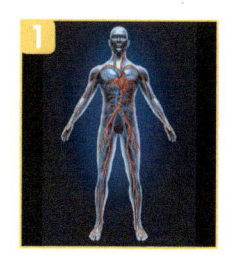

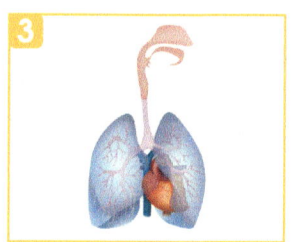

学习生词 Words and Expressions 🎧 2-1

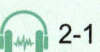

1	快速	kuàisù	*adj.*	rapid
2	评估	pínggū	*v.*	assess
3	突发	tūfā	*v.*	suddenly happen
4	马上	mǎshàng	*adv.*	immediately
5	打	dǎ	*v.*	call; phone
6	医院	yīyuàn	*n.*	hospital
7	的	de	*aux.*	(used with an adjective or attribute phrase)
8	电话	diànhuà	*n.*	phone
9	和	hé	*conj.*	and
10	意识	yìshí	*n.*	awareness

11

11	气道	qìdào	n.	airway
12	呼吸	hūxī	v.	breathe
13	循环	xúnhuán	v.	circulate
14	对	duì	prep.	to
15	呼叫	hūjiào	v.	call
16	疼痛	téngtòng	adj.	painful
17	没	méi	v.	don't have
18	反应	fǎnyìng	n.	response

词语练习　Words Exercises

1. 看图说词。 Look at the pictures and say the words.

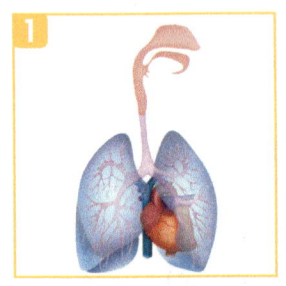

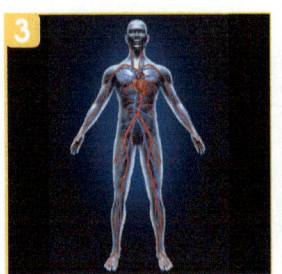

2. 朗读短语。 Read the phrases aloud.

突发急症　　打电话　　快速评估

有反应　　没有反应　　马上抢救

第 2 课 | 快速评估

学习课文 Text 2-2

快速评估
Kuàisù pínggū

病人突发急症，我们要马上打医院的急救电话。医生和护士快速评估病人的意识、气道、呼吸和循环。病人对呼叫和疼痛没反应，要马上抢救。

Rapid Assessment

If the patient has a sudden emergency, we must immediately call the hospital's emergency number. Doctors and nurses quickly assess the patient's awareness, airways, breathing, and circulation. If the patient has no response to calls and pain, immediate rescue is needed.

课文练习 Text Exercises

1. 判断正误。True or false.

① 病人突发急症，我们要马上打急救电话。

13

② 护士和医生要快速评估病人。

③ 医生只（zhǐ，only）评估病人的意识和气道。

④ 病人对呼叫没反应，不用马上抢救。

2. 选词填空。 Fill in the blanks with the correct words.

> A 急救　　　　B 气道　　　　C 循环　　　　D 疼痛

① 病人突发急症，要马上打医院的_____电话。

② 快速评估是评估病人的意识、气道、呼吸和_____。

③ 快速评估包括（bāokuò，include）病人的意识、循环、呼吸和_____。

④ 病人对呼叫和_____没反应，要马上抢救。

学习语法 Grammar

语法点 1 Grammar Point 1

结构助词：的　Structural particle: 的

结构助词"的"可以放在名词、代词与被修饰的名词之间，形成一个偏正结构，表示所属。常用结构：A + 的 + B。

The structural particle "的" can be placed between nouns, pronouns, and the noun being modified to form an attributive structure, indicating belonging. The common structure is: A + 的 + B.

例句：
1. bìngrén de yìshí
病人的意识 the patient's awareness
2. bìngrén de qìdào
病人的气道 the patient's airway
3. bìngrén de hūxī
病人的呼吸 the patient's breathing

语法练习 1 Grammar Exercise 1

用"A + 的 + B"完成句子。Complete the sentences with "A + 的 + B".

1. 医生要快速评估_____（病人　意识　的）。
2. 护士要快速评估_____（气道　病人　的）。
3. 病人对_____（医生　呼叫　的）没有反应。
4. 医生要尽快赶到_____（的　病人　家里）。

语法点 2 Grammar Point 2

连词：和　Conjunction: 和

连词"和"连接并列的词语或短语。
The conjunction "和" connects words or phrases in parallel.

例句：
1. Yīshēng hé hùshi yào jǐnkuài gǎndào bìngrén jiāli.
医生和护士要尽快赶到病人家里。Doctors and nurses should arrive at the patient's home as soon as possible.
2. Yīshēng kuàisù pínggū bìngrén de yìshí, qìdào, hūxī hé xúnhuán.
医生快速评估病人的意识、气道、呼吸和循环。The doctor rapidly assesses the patient's awareness, airways, breathing, and circulation.
3. Bìngrén duì hūjiào hé téngtòng méi fǎnyìng.
病人对呼叫和疼痛没反应。The patient has no response to calls and pain.

语法练习 2 Grammar Exercise 2

把"和"放在句中合适的位置。Put "和" in the right place in the sentence.

1. 医生____护士____抢救____病人。

2. 病人____对____呼叫____疼痛____没反应。

3. 救护车、____医生____护士要尽快赶到病人家里。

4. 快速评估病人的____意识、____气道、____呼吸____循环。

汉字书写 Writing Chinese Characters

wǔ
五 五 五 五 五
五 五 五 五 五

liù
六 六 六 六
六 六 六 六 六

qī
七 七
七 七 七 七 七

bā
八 八
八 八 八 八 八

职业拓展 Career Insight

The Pre-hospital Emergency Mode in China

Shanghai adopts an independent operation mode for pre-hospital emergency treatment, with independent pre-hospital emergency medical institutions, personnel, emergency equipment, and command and dispatch operation system. The pre-hospital emergency service function in Shanghai has gradually shifted from the original "simple transportation" to a "combination of pre-hospital emergency and rapid transportation" model. The municipal medical emergency center and each suburban (county) emergency center (station) are respectively responsible for the regional daily emergency work. In case of a major catastrophic event, the city's pre-hospital emergency resources are under the unified command and transfer of the municipal medical emergency center. This model is more suitable for the development of large cities and is currently adopted by most cities in China.

小结 Summary

词语 Words

朗读词语。Read the words aloud.

呼吸	循环	意识
反应	急症	评估

语法 Grammar

朗读短语。Read the phrases aloud.

医院的急救电话	病人的意识
呼吸和循环	呼叫和疼痛

课文理解 Text Comprehension

根据课文内容选词填空。Fill in the blanks with correct words according to the text.

A 循环　　　　B 气道　　　　C 马上　　　　D 疼痛

医生和护士要快速评估病人的意识、_____、呼吸和_____。病人对呼叫和_____没反应，要_____抢救。

第3课 Lesson 3

病情分类
Bìngqíng fēnlèi
Disease Condition Classification

复习 Revision

朗读句子。Read the sentences aloud.

1. 病人突发急症。
2. 马上打医院的急救电话。
3. 快速评估病人的意识、气道、呼吸和循环。
4. 病人对呼叫和疼痛没反应。

热身 Warming Up

看图选词。Look at the pictures and choose the correct words.

A 绿色 lǜsè green   B 红色 hóngsè red
C 黑色 hēisè black   D 黄色 huángsè yellow

学习生词 Words and Expressions 🎧 3-1

1	病情	bìngqíng	n	disease condition
2	分类	fēnlèi	v.	classify
2	使用	shǐyòng	v.	use
3	法	fǎ	n.	method
4	给	gěi	prep.	to
6	分	fēn	v.	divide
7	为	wéi	v.	become
8	个	gè	measure word	(used before a noun)
9	等级	děngjí	n.	level
10	轻度	qīngdù	adj.	mild
11	中度	zhōngdù	adj.	moderate

第 3 课 | 病情分类

12	重度	zhòngdù	*adj.*	severe
13	死亡	sǐwáng	*v.*	die
14	标记	biāojì	*v.*	mark
15	绿色	lǜsè	*n.*	green
16	黄色	huángsè	*n.*	yellow
17	红色	hóngsè	*n.*	red
18	黑色	hēisè	*n.*	black

词语练习 Words Exercises

1. 看图说词。 Look at the pictures and say the words.

2. 朗读词语。 Read the words aloud.

轻度　　　　中度　　　　重度

死亡　　　绿——绿色　　黄——黄色

红——红色　　黑——黑色

21

学习课文 Text 🎧 3-2

病情分类
Bìngqíng fēnlèi

使用 START 分类法给病情分类。病情分为四个等级:轻度、中度、重度、死亡,标记为绿色、黄色、红色、黑色。

Disease Condition Classification

Use the START classification method to classify the disease condition. The disease conditions are classified into four levels: mild, moderate, severe, and death, marked as green, yellow, red, and black.

课文练习 Text Exercises

1. 判断正误。True or false.

① START 是病情分类法。

② 病情分为四个等级。

③ 绿色标记中度病人。

④ 红色标记死亡病人。

2. 选词填空。 Fill in the blanks with the correct words.

① 使用_____分类法给病情分类。

　A START　　　　B SARTT　　　　C TSART

② 病情分为_____个等级。

　A 4　　　　　　B 3　　　　　　　C 2

③ 轻度病情标记为_____。

　A 黄色　　　　　B 绿色　　　　　C 红色

④ 重度病情标记为_____。

　A 红色　　　　　B 黄色　　　　　C 黑色

学习语法 Grammar

语法点 1 Grammar Point 1

特殊句型：连动句 1 Special sentence pattern: the sentence with a serial verb construction 1

一个句子中两个谓语动词共用一个主语，叫连动句。本课所学的连动句中第一个动词短语是第二个动词短语的方式。

The sentence in which two predicate verbs share the same subject is called the sentence with a serial verb construction. In the sentence of this lesson, the first verb phrase is the manner of the latter verb phrase.

例句：① 使用 START 分类法给 病情 分类。Use the START
　　　　Shǐyòng　　　　　fēnlèi fǎ gěi bìngqíng fēnlèi.

classification method to classify the disease condition.

2 使用 黄色 标记中度 病情。Use yellow to mark the moderate condition.
   Shǐyòng huángsè biāojì zhōngdù bìngqíng.

3 护士呼叫病人评估病人的意识。The nurse calls the patient to assess his awareness.
   Hùshì hūjiào bìngrén pínggū bìngrén de yìshí.

语法练习 1 Grammar Exercise 1

连线组句。Match the two columns to make sentences.

1 护士呼叫病人　　　　　　　　　　标记重读病情

2 使用红色　　　　　　　　　　　　给病情分类

3 使用绿色　　　　　　　　　　　　评估病人的意识

4 使用 START 分类法　　　　　　　标记轻度病情

语法点 2 Grammar Point 2

短语：数量短语　Phrase: the numeral-measure word phrase

数量短语的常用结构是：数词＋量词＋名词。
The structure of common numeral-measure word phrase is: numeral + measure word + noun.

10 以内的基本数词有：The basic numbers within 10 are:

1	2	3	4	5	6	7	8	9	10
一	二	三	四	五	六	七	八	九	十
yī	èr	sān	sì	wǔ	liù	qī	bā	jiǔ	shí

量词表示名词的个体单位。不同的名词，与其搭配的量词不同。"个"是最常见的量词。"名"和"位"用于人，"位"有尊敬的意味。
The measure words represent individual units of nouns. Different nouns are matched by

different measure words. "个" is the most common measure word. "名" and "位" are used for people, and "位" shows respect.

例句：
1. 病情分为四个等级。The disease conditions are classified into four levels.
2. 这位医生是王医生。The doctor is Dr. Wang.
3. 我要打一个电话。I have to make a phone call.

语法练习 2　Grammar Exercise 2

用 "数词+量词+名词" 完成句子。Complete the sentences with "numeral + measure word + noun".

1. 我是_____（一　护士　名）。
2. 王天是_____（位　一　医生）。
3. 病情分为_____（等级　四　个）。
4. 用_____（四　颜色　个）标记病情。

汉字书写　Writing Chinese Characters

jiǔ
九

wán
丸

ér 儿 儿
儿 儿 儿 儿 儿

jǐ 几 几
几 几 几 几 几

文化拓展 Culture Insight

Ancient Chinese Emergency Medicine

In ancient China, the struggle against natural disasters, accidental injuries, and diseases led to the development of emergency medicine. Over 2,000 years ago, the *Huangdi Neijing* (*Yellow Emperor's Inner Classic*), a foundational text in traditional Chinese medicine, recorded medical theories that still serve as a cornerstone of the practice today.

Around 1,700 years ago, the renowned physician Zhang Zhongjing creatively introduced the concept of artificial respiration to save patients who had hanged themselves. Over 1,300 years ago, Sun Simiao compiled an extensive record of 800 types of drugs and treatments for various conditions, including internal and external ailments, gynecological issues, infant care, infectious diseases, and emergencies.

These rich medical traditions reflect the unique insights and practical experiences of ancient Chinese practitioners, laying the foundation for the development of emergency medicine and critical nursing.

第 3 课 | 病情分类

小结 Summary

词语 Words

朗读词语。Read the words aloud.

| 分类法 | 病情 | 轻度 |
| 中度 | 重度 | 死亡 |

语法 Grammar

朗读句子。Read the sentences aloud.

1. 使用 START 分类法给病情分类。
2. 使用红色标记重度病情。
3. 病情分为四个等级。
4. 使用四个颜色标记病情等级。

课文理解 Text Comprehension

根据提示，说明 START 病情分类法。Explain the START classification method according to the hints.

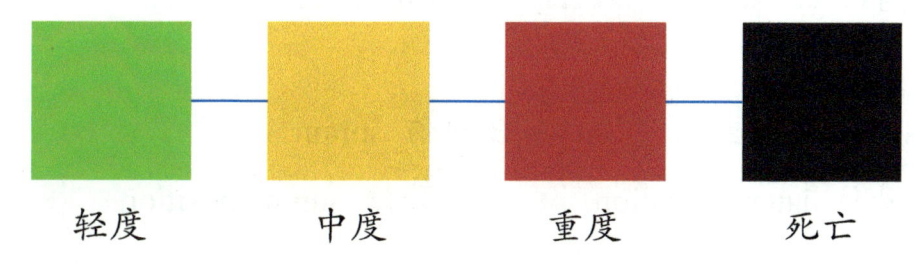

| 轻度 | 中度 | 重度 | 死亡 |

使用 START 分类法给病情分类。轻度病情标记为……

27

第4课 Lesson 4

摆好体位 Bǎihǎo tǐwèi
Positioning

复习 Revision

朗读词语。Read the words aloud.

轻度	中度	重度	死亡
绿色	黄色	红色	黑色
评估病情	抢救病人	没有呼吸、意识	

热身 Warming Up

看图选词。Look at the pictures and choose the correct words.

A 心跳 xīntiào heartbeat
B 扭伤 niǔshāng sprain
C 侧卧位 cèwòwèi lateral position
D 仰卧位 yǎngwòwèi supine position

第 4 课 | 摆好体位

学习生词　Words and Expressions　🎧 4-1

1	摆好	bǎihǎo	*v.*	position
2	体位	tǐwèi	*n.*	posture
3	后	hòu	*n.*	after
4	先	xiān	*adv.*	first
5	再	zài	*adv.*	then
6	进行	jìnxíng	*v.*	proceed
7	有	yǒu	*v.*	have
8	心跳	xīntiào	*v.*	heartbeat
9	也	yě	*adv.*	too
10	采取	cǎiqǔ	*v.*	take
11	仰卧位	yǎngwòwèi	*n.*	supine position
12	侧卧位	cèwòwèi	*n.*	lateral position
13	扭伤	niǔshāng	*v.*	sprain
14	抬高	táigāo	*v.*	raise
15	患肢	huànzhī	*n.*	affected extremity

29

词语练习 Words Exercises

1. 看图说词。Look at the pictures and say the words.

2. 朗读短语。Read the phrases aloud.

采取仰卧位　　采取侧卧位　　摆好体位　　抬高患肢

有心跳　　没有呼吸　　也没有意识

学习课文　Text　8-2

Bǎihǎo tǐwèi
摆好体位

Pínggū bìngrén de bìngqíng hòu, xiān bǎihǎo tǐwèi, zài
评估病人的病情后，先摆好体位，再
jìnxíng qiǎngjiù. Méiyǒu hūxī, méiyǒu xīntiào, yě méiyǒu yìshi de
进行抢救。没有呼吸、没有心跳，也没有意识的
bìngrén, cǎiqǔ yǎngwòwèi; yǒu hūxī, yǒu xīntiào, méiyǒu yìshi
病人，采取仰卧位；有呼吸、有心跳、没有意识

de bìngrén cǎiqǔ cèwòwèi; niǔshāng de bìngrén, táigāo huànzhī.
的病人采取侧卧位；扭伤的病人，抬高患肢。

Positioning

After assessing the patient's disease condition, first position him/her properly, then proceed with rescue. The patient without breathing, heartbeat, or awareness should take a supine position; The patient with breathing, heartbeat, and unconsciousness should take a lateral position; The patient with a sprain should raise his/her affected extremity.

课文练习 Text Exercises

1. 判断正误。True or false.

① 先抢救，再评估病情。

② 先摆好体位，再抢救。

③ 没有意识的病人，采取侧卧位。

④ 没有呼吸的病人，抬高患肢。

2. 选词填空。Fill in the blanks with the correct words.

① 评估病人的_____后，摆好体位。

   A 病情   B 呼吸   C 心跳

② 先摆好_____，再进行抢救。

   A 体位   B 扭伤   C 抬高

3 没有呼吸、没有心跳，也没有意识的病人，_____。

　A 采取仰卧位　　B 采取侧卧位　　C 抬高患肢

4 有呼吸、有心跳、没有意识的病人_____。

　A 采取仰卧位　　B 采取侧卧位　　C 抬高患肢

学习语法 Grammar

语法点 1　Grammar Point 1

承接复句：先……再……　　Successive complex sentence: 先 … 再 …

"先……再……"连接两个动作，表示动作的先后次序。

"先 … 再 …" connects two actions, indicating the order of actions.

例句：

1 先摆好体位，再进行抢救。First position the patient properly, then proceed with rescue.

2 先评估病人，再抢救。First assess the patient, then rescue him.

3 先打急救电话，再去（go to）医院。Make an emergency call first, then go to the hospital.

语法练习 1　Grammar Exercise 1

用"先……再……"完成句子。Connect sentences with "先 … 再 …".

1 摆好体位　　进行抢救　　_____

2. 评估病人　　抢救　　_____

3. 认识急救　　学习急救　_____

4. 呼叫病人　　抢救　　_____

语法点 2 Grammar Point 2

特殊句型：“有”字句 Special sentence pattern: the 有-sentence

动词"有"可以表示主语领有或具有。"有"的否定形式是"没有"。
The verb "有" can indicate that the subject possesses or has. The negative form of "有" is "没有".

例句：
1. Bìngrén yǒu hūxī.
   病人有呼吸。The patient is breathing.
2. Bìngrén méiyǒu xīntiào.
   病人没有心跳。The patient has no heartbeat.
3. Bìngrén duì hūjiào hé téngtòng méiyǒu fǎnyìng.
   病人对呼叫和疼痛没有反应。The patient has no response to calls and pain.

语法练习 2 Grammar Exercise 2

把肯定句改成否定句，或者把否定句改成肯定句。Change the affirmative sentence to a negative sentence, or the negative sentence to an affirmative sentence.

1. 病人没有呼吸。_____

2. 病人有心跳。_____

3. 病人对呼叫和疼痛有反应。_____

4. 病人没有意识。_____

汉字书写 Writing Chinese Characters

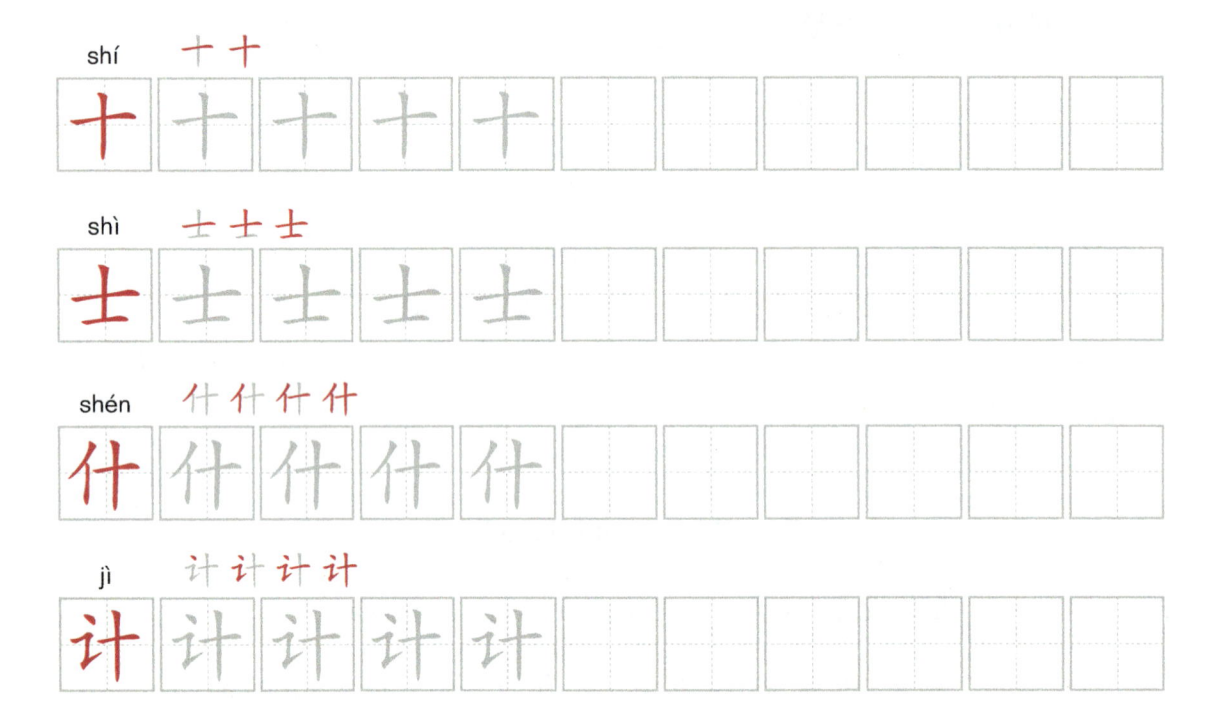

shí
十　十 十
十　十 十 十 十

shì
士　士 士 士
士　士 士 士 士

shén
什　什 什 什 什
什　什 什 什 什

jì
计　计 计 计 计
计　计 计 计 计

职业拓展 Career Insight

The Color of Hospital Nursing

In modern hospitals, color is used as a tool for psychological intervention and patient treatment. Colors are generally classified into warm and cool categories. Warm colors have the ability to relieve psychological stress and reduce fear, while cool colors help promote clear thinking, soothe the mind, and support smooth breathing.

Colors have a soothing and compensatory psychological effect. When applied appropriately, they can help create a stable and safe healthcare environment for patients, allowing them to receive treatment in a more comfortable setting. The positive influence of the environment can alleviate the anxiety of patients and families, fostering a peaceful atmosphere that improves the overall quality of nursing care.

小结 Summary

词语 Words

朗读词语。Read the words aloud.

摆好体位	进行抢救	有心跳
仰卧位/侧卧位	扭伤	抬高患肢

语法 Grammar

朗读句子。Read the sentences aloud.

1. 先摆好体位，再进行抢救。
2. 病人没有呼吸、没有心跳，也没有意识。
3. 病人有呼吸、有心跳、没有意识。
4. 先抬高病人患肢，再进行抢救。

课文理解 Text Comprehension

选词填空。Fill in the blanks with the correct words.

| A 侧卧位 | B 仰卧位 | C 抬高患肢 |

病情	体位
没有呼吸、没有心跳，也没有意识	
有呼吸、有心跳、没有意识	
扭伤	

第5课 急救要点
Lesson 5　Jíjiù yàodiǎn
Key Points of First Aid

复习 Revision

选词填空。Fill in the blanks with the correct words.

| A 抬高患肢 | B 病情 | C 体位 | D 侧卧位 |

1. 要先评估病人的_____。
2. 先摆好_____再进行抢救。
3. 有呼吸和心跳、没有意识的病人采取_____。
4. 扭伤的病人_____。

热身 Warming Up

看图选词。Look at the pictures and choose the correct words.

A 心电监护 xīndiàn jiānhù electrocardiogram monitoring　　B 静脉 jìngmài vein
C 移动 yídòng move　　D 药物 yàowù medicine　　E 脊柱 jǐzhù spine　　F 通路 tōnglù access

急救护理（基里巴斯版） 初级篇

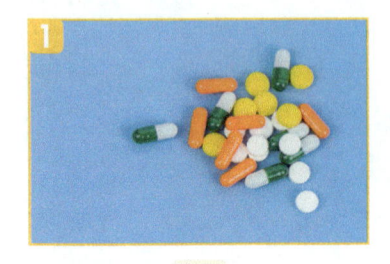

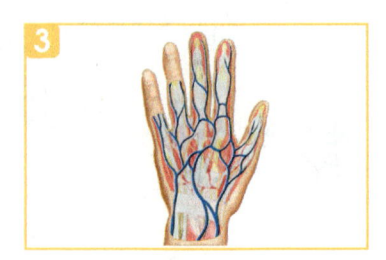

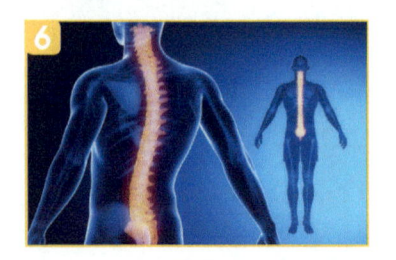

学习生词 Words and Expressions 🎧 5-1

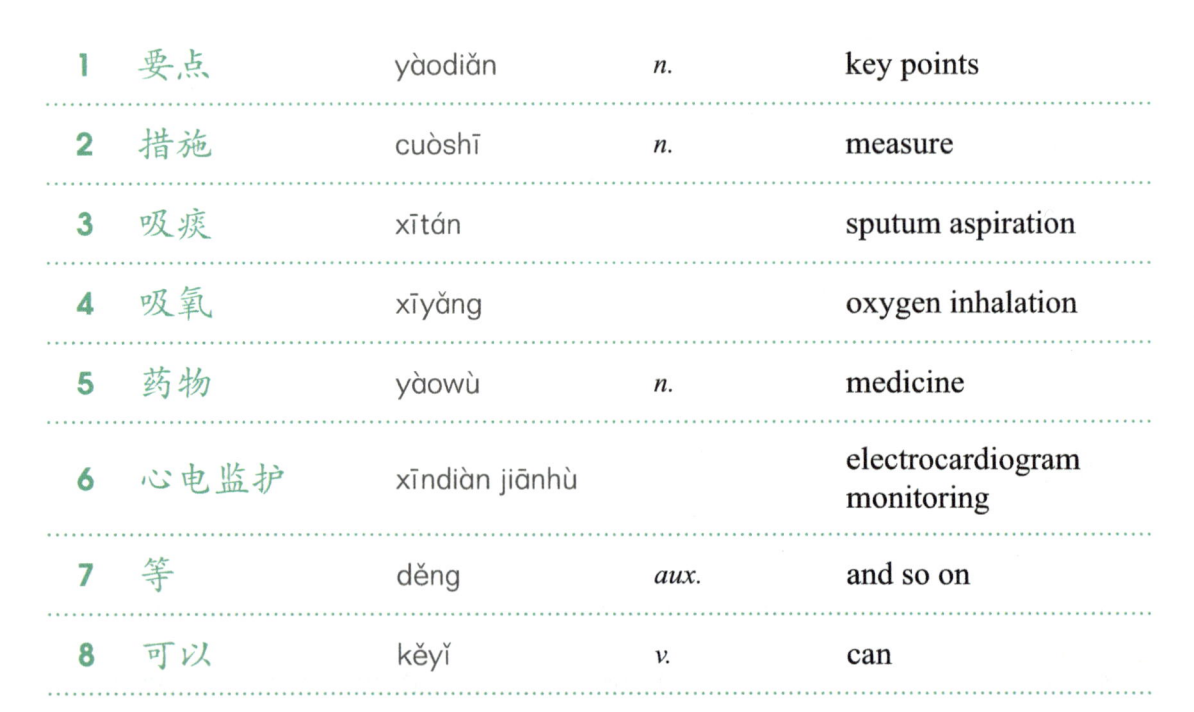

1	要点	yàodiǎn	*n.*	key points
2	措施	cuòshī	*n.*	measure
3	吸痰	xītán		sputum aspiration
4	吸氧	xīyǎng		oxygen inhalation
5	药物	yàowù	*n.*	medicine
6	心电监护	xīndiàn jiānhù		electrocardiogram monitoring
7	等	děng	*aux.*	and so on
8	可以	kěyǐ	*v.*	can

第 5 课 | 急救要点

9	维持	wéichí	v.	maintain
10	功能	gōngnéng	n.	function
11	对于	duìyú	prep.	with regard to
12	休克	xiūkè	v.	shock
13	建立	jiànlì	v.	establish
14	静脉通路	jìngmài tōnglù		venous access
15	脊柱	jǐzhù	n.	spine
16	损伤	sǔnshāng	v.	damage
17	不	bù	adv.	not
18	移动	yídòng	v.	move

词语练习 Words Exercises

1. 看图说词。 Look at the pictures and say the words.

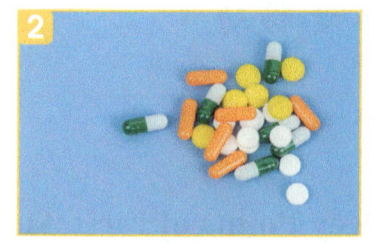

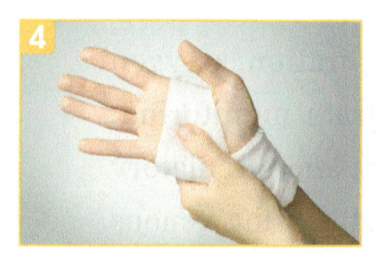

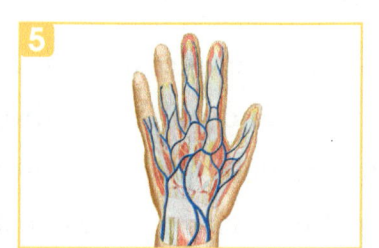

39

2. 朗读短语。Read the phrases aloud.

- 急救措施
- 使用药物
- 心电监护
- 维持呼吸
- 循环功能
- 建立静脉通路

学习课文 Text 5-2

急救要点
Jíjiù yàodiǎn

急救措施有吸痰、吸氧、使用药物和心电监护等，可以维持病人的呼吸和循环功能。对于休克的病人，建立静脉通路。对于脊柱损伤的病人，不要移动。

Key Points of First Aid

First aid measures include sputum aspiration, oxygen inhalation, medication, and electrocardiogram monitoring, which can maintain the patient's respiratory and circulatory functions. For the patient with a shock, establish the venous access. For the patient with a spinal injury, do not move.

第 5 课 | 急救要点

课文练习 Text Exercises

1. 判断正误。True or false.

① 心电监护不是急救措施。

② 吸痰等急救措施可以维持病人的呼吸和循环功能。

③ 对于休克的病人，使用吸氧措施急救。

④ 不要移动脊柱损伤的病人。

2. 选词填空。Fill in the blanks with the correct words.

| A 静脉 | B 移动 | C 药物 | D 循环 |

① 急救措施有吸痰、吸氧、使用_____和心电监护等。

② 急救可以维持病人的呼吸和_____功能。

③ 对于休克的病人，建立_____通路。

④ 对于脊柱损伤的病人，不要_____。

学习语法 Grammar

语法点 1 Grammar Point 1

其他助词：等　Other particle: 等

助词"等"用在列举的事项后面，表示列举未尽。
The particle "等" is used after the listed items to indicate that it is not fully listed.

例句：

1. 急救措施有吸痰、吸氧、使用药物和心电监护等。
Jíjiù cuòshī yǒu xītán, xīyǎng, shǐyòng yàowù hé xīndiàn jiānhù děng.
First aid measures include sputum aspiration, oxygen inhalation, medication, and electrocardiogram monitoring.

2. 病情分为轻度、中度、重度等。The disease conditions are classified into mild, moderate, severe, death, etc.
Bìngqíng fēn wéi qīngdù, zhōngdù, zhòngdù děng.

3. 病情标记为绿色、黄色、红色等。The disease conditions are marked as green, yellow, red, black, etc.
Bìngqíng biāojì wéi lǜsè, huángsè, hóngsè děng.

语法练习 1 Grammar Exercise 1

把"等"放在句中合适的位置。Place "等" in the right place in the sentence.

1. 病情____分为____轻度、中度、____重度、死亡____。
2. 病情标记____为____绿色、黄色、____红色、黑色____。
3. 急救措施____有吸痰、____吸氧、____使用药物和心电监护____。
4. 要____快速评估____病人的意识、气道、呼吸____和循环____。

语法点 2 Grammar Point 2

介词：对于　Preposition: 对于

介词"对于"引出对象或事物的关系者。
The preposition "对于" introduces the target or the related subject.

例句：

1. 对于休克的病人，建立静脉通路。For the patient with a shock, establish the venous access.
Duìyú xiūkè de bìngrén, jiànlì jìngmài tōnglù.

第 5 课 | 急救要点

2. Duìyú jǐzhù sǔnshāng de bìngrén, búyào yídòng.
   对于脊柱损伤的病人，不要移动。For the patient with a spinal injury, do not move.

3. Duìyú bìngrén, wǒmen kěyǐ jìnxíng xīndiàn jiānhù.
   对于病人，我们可以进行心电监护。For patients, we can conduct electrocardiogram monitoring.

语法练习 2 Grammar Exercise 2

用"对于"完成句子。Complete the sentences with "对于".

1. 脊柱损伤的病人　　不要移动

   _____

2. 休克的病人　　建立静脉通路

   _____

3. 对呼叫和疼痛没有反应的病人　　要马上抢救

   _____

4. 扭伤的病人　　抬高他的患肢

   _____

汉字书写 Writing Chinese Characters

rén
人

cóng 从 从从从从
从 从 从 从 从

zhòng 众 众众众众众众
众 众 众 众 众

gè 个 个个个
个 个 个 个 个

文化拓展 Culture Insight

Tai Chi — An Internal Chinese Martial Art

The philosophy of Tai Chi is rooted in the concept of *yin* and *yang*, which encompasses both the static and dynamic, as well as the fast and slow. In Chinese thought, dynamic energy is contained within static, and fast energy is contained within slow. Tai Chi represents the harmonious combination of these energies.

Its fighting principle involves maneuvering the flow of internal energy to achieve both speed and power. However, the most important function of Tai Chi is to experience the balance of static and dynamic energies in nature and life. It aims to cultivate harmony between one's heart, body, and nature.

第 5 课 | 急救要点

小结 Summary

词语 Words

朗读词语。Read the words aloud.

| 吸痰 | 吸氧 | 休克 |
| 心电监护 | 静脉通路 | 脊柱损伤 |

语法 Grammar

朗读句子。Read the sentences aloud.

1. 急救措施有吸痰、吸氧等。
2. 急救措施有使用药物和心电监护等。
3. 对于休克的病人，建立静脉通路。
4. 对于脊柱损伤病人，不要移动。

课文理解 Text Comprehension

选词填空。Fill in the blanks with the correct words.

A 吸氧　　B 移动　　C 休克　　D 心电监护　　D 循环功能

急救措施有吸痰、_____、使用药物和_____等，可以维持病人的呼吸和_____。对于_____的病人，建立静脉通路。对于脊柱损伤的病人，不要_____。

45

Unit 2

第二单元

Jízhěn fēnzhěn
急诊分诊
Emergency Triage

第6课 Lesson 6

急诊科
Jízhěnkē
Emergency Department

复习 Revision

朗读短语。Read the phrases aloud.

- 吸痰
- 吸氧
- 使用药物
- 维持呼吸
- 维持循环功能
- 建立静脉通路
- 脊柱损伤

热身 Warming Up

看图选词。Look at the pictures and choose the correct words.

A 分诊处 (fēnzhěnchù) triage area
B 监护 (jiānhù) monitor
C 观察 (guānchá) observe
D 中间 (zhōngjiān) middle

第 6 课 | 急诊科

学习生词 Words and Expressions 🎧 6-1

1	急诊科	jízhěnkē	n.	emergency department
2	分诊处	fēnzhěnchù	n.	triage area
3	在	zài	v.	be located in
4	大厅	dàtīng	n.	lobby
5	中间	zhōngjiān	n.	middle
6	轻症	qīngzhèng	n.	mild symptom
7	登记	dēngjì	v.	register
8	基本	jīběn	adj.	basic
9	信息	xìnxī	n.	information

10	安排	ānpái	v.	arrange
11	就诊	jiùzhěn	v.	visit (hospital)
12	顺序	shùnxù	n.	order
13	旁边	pángbiān	n.	next to
14	重症监护室	zhòngzhèng jiānhùshì	n.	intensive care unit
15	观察室	guāncháshì	n.	observation room
16	后边	hòubian	n.	back

词语练习 Words Exercises

1. 看图说词。Look at the pictures and say the words.

2. 朗读词语搭配。Read the collocations aloud.

登记信息　　安排顺序　　轻症病人　　重症监护

学习课文 Text 🎧 6-2

急诊科 Jízhěnkē

分诊处在急诊科大厅中间。对于轻症病人,分诊护士登记病人的基本信息,安排就诊顺序。分诊处的旁边是抢救室。重症监护室在观察室的后边。

Emergency Department

The triage area is located in the middle of the emergency department lobby. For patients with mild symptoms, the triage nurse registers their basic information and arrange the order of visits. The emergency treatment room is next to the triage area. The intensive care unit is located behind the observation room.

课文练习 Text Exercises

1. 判断正误。 True or false.

① 急诊科大厅中间是分诊处。

② 对于轻症病人，分诊护士马上安排就诊。

③ 抢救室在分诊处的旁边。

④ 重症监护室在观察室的旁边。

2. 选词填空。 Fill in the blanks with the correct words.

| A 后边 | B 旁边 | C 中间 | D 分诊处 |

① 分诊处在急诊科大厅的_____。

② 抢救室在分诊处的_____。

③ 重症监护室在观察室的_____。

④ 护士在_____安排病人的就诊顺序。

学习语法 Grammar

语法点 1 Grammar Point 1

动词：在 Verb: 在

"在"是动词时，在句中做谓语。"人/事物＋在＋地方"表示人或事物的处所、位置。
When "在" is used as a verb, it serves as the predicate in the sentence. "Someone/something + 在 + location" indicates the place or location of the person or the thing.

例句：

① Fēnzhěnchù zài jízhěnkē dàtīng.
分诊处在急诊科大厅。The triage area is located in the emergency department lobby.

② Qiǎngjiùshì zài fēnzhěnchù de pángbiān.
抢救室在分诊处的旁边。The emergency treatment room is next to the triage area.

3. Zhòngzhèng jiānhùshì zài guāncháshì de hòubian. 重症监护室在观察室的后边。The intensive care unit is located behind the observation room.

语法练习 1 Grammar Exercise 1

按照正确的语序连词成句。Make sentences in correct orders with the given words or phrases.

1. ①抢救室　②在　③分诊处的旁边

   _____

2. ①分诊处　②在　③急诊科大厅

   _____

3. ①重症监护室　②在　③观察室的后边

   _____

4. ①医生　②在　③病人家里

   _____

语法点 2 Grammar Point 2

方位名词：中间 / 旁边 / 后边　Nouns of locality: 中间 / 旁边 / 后边

方位词是表示方向或位置的词。汉语的方位词有：

Nouns of locality are words that indicate location or position. Chinese nouns of locality are:

shàng 上 up	xià 下 down	zuǒ 左 left	yòu 右 right	qián 前 front	hòu 后 back	zhōng 中 middle	páng 旁 side
shàngbian 上边 upside	xiàbian 下边 downside	zuǒbian 左边 left side	yòubian 右边 right side	qiánbian 前边 frontside	hòubian 后边 backside	zhōngjiān 中间 middle	pángbiān 旁边 beside

53

例句：
1. Qiǎngjiùshì zài fēnzhěnchù de pángbiān.
抢救室在分诊处的旁边。The emergency treatment room is next to the triage area.

2. Zhòngzhèng jiānhùshì zài guāncháshì de hòubian.
重症监护室在观察室的后边。The intensive care unit is located behind the observation room.

3. Fēnzhěnchù zài jízhěnkē dàtīng zhōngjiān.
分诊处在急诊科大厅中间。The triage area is located in the middle of the emergency department lobby.

语法练习 2 Grammar Exercise 2

看图，选词填空。Look at the picture and fill in the blanks with the correct words.

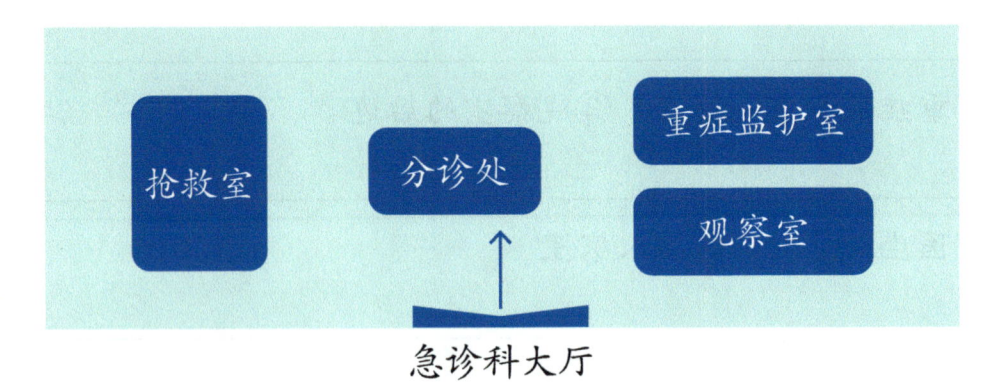

抢救室　　分诊处　　重症监护室　　观察室

急诊科大厅

A 中间　　　　B 旁边　　　　C 后边

1. 分诊处在急诊大厅的_____。

2. 抢救室在分诊处的_____。

3. 观察室在分诊处的_____。

4. 重症观察室在观察室的_____。

汉字书写 Writing Chinese Characters

yòu
又 又
又 又 又 又 又

shuāng
双 双 双 双
双 双 双 双 双

jǐn
仅 仅 仅 仅
仅 仅 仅 仅 仅

fǎn
反 反 反 反
反 反 反 反 反

职业拓展 Career Insight

First Aid Centers in China

In China, emergency centers are linked with various accident alarm stations, public transportation systems, subways, airports, and other departments to facilitate emergency command and unified dispatch operations. The first aid centers are supported by sub-centers and aid stations, forming a comprehensive emergency network system.

According to Chinese regulations, the first aid coverage radius in urban areas should be no more than 5 km, while in rural areas, it should be no more than 15 km. Response times are required to be within 10 to 15 minutes in urban areas and no longer than 30 minutes in suburban areas.

小结 Summary

词语 Words

朗读词语。Read the words aloud.

急诊科	分诊处	观察室
轻症—重症	重症监护室	就诊

语法 Grammar

朗读句子。Read the sentences aloud.

1. 分诊处在急诊科大厅中间。
2. 分诊处的旁边是抢救室。
3. 重症监护室在观察室的后边。
4. 护士在分诊处。

课文理解 Text Comprehension

根据提示说一说急诊科的布局，并说明分诊护士怎么分诊。Explain the layout of the emergency department and how the triage nurses conduct triage according to the hints.

抢救室　　分诊处　　重症监护室　　观察室

急诊科大厅

1. 分诊处在……
2. 分诊护士……

第7课 Lesson 7

分诊方法 Fēnzhěn fāngfǎ
Triage Method

复习 Revision

朗读句子。Read the sentences aloud.

1. 护士登记轻症病人的基本信息。
2. 护士安排就诊顺序。
3. 分诊处在急诊科大厅中间。
4. 重症监护室在观察室的后边。

热身 Warming Up

看图选词。Look at the pictures and choose the correct words.

A 体征 tǐzhēng sign
B 生命 shēngmìng life
C 分钟 fēnzhōng minute
D 危险 wēixiǎn danger
E 出血 chūxiě hemorrhage
F 腹痛 fùtòng abdominal pain

学习生词 Words and Expressions 🎧 7-1

1	方法	fāngfǎ	n.	method
2	级	jí	measure word	level
3	生命	shēngmìng	n.	life
4	体征	tǐzhēng	n.	sign
5	稳定	wěndìng	adj.	stable
6	随时	suíshí	adv.	anytime
7	危险	wēixiǎn	n.	risk
8	例如	lìrú	v.	such as

第 7 课 | 分诊方法

9	可能	kěnéng	adv.	may
10	活动性	huódòngxìng	n.	activity
11	出血	chūxiě	v.	hemorrhage
12	监护	jiānhù	v.	monitor
13	分钟	fēnzhōng	n.	minute
14	内	nèi	n.	within
15	治疗	zhìliáo	v.	treat
16	急	jí	adj.	acute
17	腹痛	fùtòng		abdominal pain

词语练习 Words Exercises

1. 看图说词。 Look at the pictures and say the words.

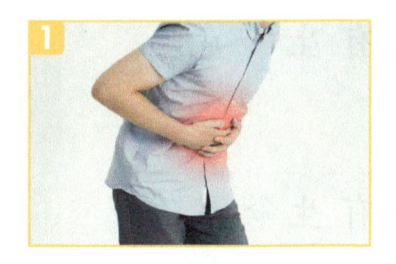

2. 朗读短语。Read the phrases aloud.

- 一级
- 二级
- 三级
- 四级
- 生命体征
- 生命危险
- 生命体征稳定
- 生命体征不稳定
- 病情急
- 病情不急

学习课文 Text 7-2

分诊方法 Fēnzhěn fāngfǎ

Bìngrén kěyǐ fēnzhěn wéi sì jí:
病人可以分诊为四级：

Yī jí: Shēngmìng tǐzhēng bù wěndìng, suíshí yǒu shēngmìng wēixiǎn, lìrú xiūkè. Yào mǎshàng qiǎngjiù.
一级：生命体征不稳定，随时有生命危险，例如休克。要马上抢救。

Èr jí: Shēngmìng tǐzhēng bù wěndìng, kěnéng yǒu shēngmìng wēixiǎn, lìrú huódòngxìng chūxiě. Yào mǎshàng jiānhù, 10 fēnzhōng nèi zhìliáo.
二级：生命体征不稳定，可能有生命危险，例如活动性出血。要马上监护，10 分钟内治疗。

Sān jí: Bìngqíng jí, shēngmìng tǐzhēng wěndìng, lìrú fùtòng. Sānshí fēnzhōng nèi zhìliáo.
三级：病情急，生命体征稳定，例如腹痛。30 分钟内治疗。

Sì jí: Bìngqíng bù jí, méiyǒu shēngmìng wēixiǎn.
四级：病情不急，没有生命危险。

Triage Method

Patients can be classified into four levels:

Level 1: Unstable vital signs that pose a life-threatening condition, such as shock. Immediate rescue is needed.

Level 2: Unstable vital signs may pose a life-threatening risk, such as active bleeding. Conduct monitoring and treatment immediately within 10 minutes.

Level 3: Acute condition with stable vital signs, such as abdominal pain. Treat within 30 minutes.

Level 4: The condition is not urgent. There is no life danger.

课文练习 Text Exercises

1. 判断正误。True or false.

1. 病人可以分诊为四级。
2. 休克是一级病人。
3. 活动性出血是二级病人。
4. 四级病情最（zuì, most）急。

2. 选词填空。Fill in the blanks with the correct words.

1. 病人分诊为_____级。

   A 2　　　　　　　　B 3　　　　　　　　C 4

2 休克是生命_____不稳定。

A 体征　　　　　　B 等级　　　　　　C 治疗

3 活动性出血是生命体征不稳定，_____有生命危险。

A 可能　　　　　　B 马上　　　　　　C 随时

4 三级病情_____内治疗。

A 10 分钟　　　　　B 20 分钟　　　　　C 30 分钟

学习语法 Grammar

语法点 1 Grammar Point 1

"不"和"没有"的区别 The differences between "不" and "没有"

"不"用在动词或形容词前面，表示对客观动作行为或性质状态的否定。"没有"用在名词前面，表示对具有或存在的否定。

"不" is used before a verb or an adjective to indicate a negation of an objective action, behavior, or state. "没有" is used before a noun to indicate a negation of possession or existence.

例句：

1. Bìngrén de shēngmìng tǐzhēng bù wěndìng.
病人的生命体征不稳定。The patient's vital signs are unstable.

2. Bìngrén méiyǒu xīntiào.
病人没有心跳。The patient has no heartbeat.

3. Bìngqíng bù jí, méiyǒu shēngmìng wēixiǎn.
病情不急，没有生命危险。The condition is not urgent and there is no life danger.

语法练习 1　Grammar Exercise 1

选题填空。Fill in the blanks with the correct words.

　　　　　　　A 不　　　　　B 没有

1. 生命体征稳定，____活动性出血。
2. 生命体征稳定，____生命危险。
3. 生命体征稳定，病情____急。
4. 生命体征____稳定，可能有生命危险。

语法点 2　Grammar Point 2

单句：形容词谓语句　Simple sentence: the sentence with adjectival predicate

用形容词作谓语，描写主语的句子叫形容词谓语句。

A sentence that uses an adjective as the predicate to describe the subject is called the sentence with adjectival predicate.

例句：
1. 生命体征稳定。(Shēngmìng tǐzhēng wěndìng.) The vital signs are stable.
2. 病情急。(Bìngqíng jí.) The condition is urgent.
3. 病人的脊柱痛。(Bìngrén de jǐzhù tòng.) The patient is suffering a spinal pain.

语法练习 2 Grammar Exercise 2

按照正确的语序连词成句。Make sentences in correct orders with the given words or phrases.

1 ①危险　②不　③病人

_____

2 ①生命体征　②稳定　③很

_____

3 ①很　②病情　③稳定

_____

4 ①不　②急　③病情

_____

汉字书写 Writing Chinese Characters

lì
力　力 力
力　力 力 力 力

bàn
办　办 办 办 办
办　办 办 办 办

nán
男　男 男 男 男 男 男
男　男 男 男 男

lìng
另　另 另 另 另
另　另 另 另 另

文化拓展 Culture Insight

Traditional Chinese Medicine: Acupuncture and Moxibustion

Acupuncture, which is called "*zhenjiu*" in Chinese, is a medical treatment that originated in China. "*Zhen*" means needles that pierce one's body. "*Jiu*" means moxibustion, a special treatment in traditional Chinese medicine. Plant leaves were once used to smoke certain parts of the human body.

Traditional Chinese medicine describes the energy flow within the human body as a network. It is called "*jingluo*". The major nodes on the network are called "*xuewei*" or an acupuncture point. Traditional Chinese doctors believe that stimulating the "*xuewei*" can promote energy circulation and expel illness. For example, having "*zhenjiu*" on "*zusanli*" can promote digestion and having "*zhenjiu*" on "*neiguan*" is good for one's heart. Chinese people have been using this medical treatment for thousands of years.

小结 Summary

词语 Words

朗读词语。Read the words aloud.

生命	体征	危险
治疗	腹痛	活动性出血

语法 Grammar

朗读句子。Read the sentences aloud.

1. 病人的生命体征不稳定。
2. 病情不急。
3. 没有生命危险。
4. 没有休克。

课文理解 Text Comprehension

填表，说说怎么分诊病人。Fill out the form and explain how to triage patients.

等级	生命体征：稳定/不稳定	生命危险：随时有/可能有	治疗方法：马上抢救/马上治疗/马上监护 治疗时间：10分钟内/30分钟内
一级			
二级			
三级			
四级			

第8课 Lesson 8

收集信息
Shōují xìnxī
Collecting Information

复习 Revision

选词填空。Fill in the blanks with the correct words.

1. 病人生命_____不稳定。

   A 体征　　　　B 病情　　　　C 信息

2. 休克病人_____有生命危险。

   A 可能　　　　B 随时　　　　C 马上

3. 活动性出血病人需要马上_____。

   A 抢救　　　　B 监护　　　　C 治疗

4. 腹痛病人生命体征_____。

   A 稳定　　　　B 急　　　　　C 危险

急救护理（基里巴斯版） 初级篇

热身 Warming Up

看图选词。Look at the pictures and choose the correct words.

A 痛 (tòng) pain	B 症状 (zhèngzhuàng) symptom
C 放射 (fàngshè) radiate	D 收集 (shōují) collect

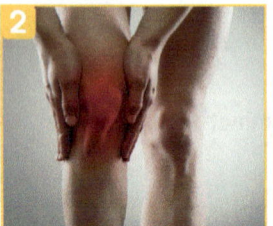

学习生词 Words and Expressions 8-1

1	收集	shōují	v.	collect
2	疼痛	téngtòng	adj.	painful
3	诱因	yòuyīn	n.	incentive
4	什么	shénme	pron.	what

68

5	症状	zhèngzhuàng	*n.*	symptom
6	性质	xìngzhì	*n.*	nature
7	放射	fàngshè	*v.*	radiate
8	部位	bùwèi	*n.*	part
9	哪里	nǎlǐ	*pron.*	where
10	程度	chéngdù	*n.*	degree
11	多少	duōshǎo	*pron.*	how much
12	无	wú	*adv.*	none
13	最	zuì	*adv.*	the most
14	严重	yánzhòng	*adj.*	severe
15	多	duō	*pron.*	how
16	久	jiǔ	*adj.*	long
17	吗	ma	*aux.*	(used at the end of an interrogative sentence)
18	反复	fǎnfù	*adv.*	repeatedly
19	出现	chūxiàn	*v.*	appear

词语练习 Words Exercises

1. 看图说词。Look at the pictures and say the words.

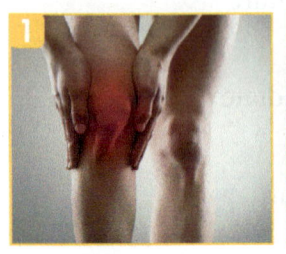

2. 朗读词语搭配。Read the collocations aloud.

PQRST 法　　收集信息　　疼痛的诱因　　疼痛程度

疼痛部位　　出现症状　　反复出现　　症状的性质

学习课文 Text　8-2

收集信息
Shōují xìnxī

可以使用 PQRST 法收集病人的信息。
Kěyǐ shǐyòng fǎ shōují bìngrén de xìnxī.

P：疼痛的诱因是什么？
Téngtòng de yòuyīn shì shénme?

Q：症状的性质是什么？
Zhèngzhuàng de xìngzhì shì shénme?

R：有放射痛吗？放射部位在哪里？
Yǒu fàngshètòng ma? Fàngshè bùwèi zài nǎli?

第 8 课 | 收集信息

S：疼痛程度是多少？（0—10，0为无，10为最严重）

T：症状有多久？反复出现吗？

Collecting Information

The PQRST method can be used to collect patients' information.

P: What are the causes of the pain?

Q: What is the nature of the symptoms?

R: Do you have any radiating pain? Where is the radiating part?

S: What is the pain severity? (0–10, 0 is none, 10 is the most severe);

T: How long have the symptoms appeared? Do they appear repeatedly?

课文练习 Text Exercises

1. 判断正误。True or false.

1　PQRST 法是收集病人信息的方法。

2　P 表示（biǎoshì, indicate）症状的性质。

3　S 为 0 表示没有疼痛。

4　T 表示症状出现的时间（shíjiān, time）。

71

2. 选词填空。Fill in the blanks with the correct words.

1. P：疼痛的_____。
   A 性质　　　　B 诱因　　　　C 程度

2. Q：症状的_____。
   A 性质　　　　B 诱因　　　　C 程度

3. S：疼痛的程度是多少？10 为最_____。
   A 严重　　　　B 轻症　　　　C 久

4. T：症状有多久？_____出现吗？
   A 马上　　　　B 反复　　　　C 久

学习语法 Grammar

语法点 1 Grammar Point 1

提问的方法：用"吗"提问　Way of asking questions: questions with "吗"

在陈述句的后面加疑问助词"吗"构成汉语的是非疑问句。

Add the interrogative modal particle "吗" after a declarative sentence to form a yes-no question.

例句：

1. Bìngrén yǒu fàngshètòng.　　Bìngrén yǒu fàngshètòng ma?
   病人有放射痛。——病人有放射痛吗？ The patient has a radiating pain.—Does the patient have a radiating pain?

2. Téngtòng fǎnfù chūxiàn.　　Téngtòng fǎnfù chūxiàn ma?
   疼痛反复出现。——疼痛反复出现吗？ The pain appears repeatedly.—Does the pain appear repeatedly?

第 8 课 | 收集信息

3. Bìngrén de shēngmìng tǐzhēng bù wěndìng. Bìngrén de shēngmìng tǐzhēng wěndìng ma?
病人的 生命 体征不稳定。——病人的 生命 体征稳定吗？ The patient's vital signs are unstable. —Are the patient's vital signs stable?

语法练习 1 Grammar Exercise 1

把陈述句改成疑问句。Change the declarative sentences into interrogative sentences.

1. 我是护士。　　　　　＿＿＿＿＿＿＿＿＿＿＿＿＿＿＿？
2. 病人有放射痛。　　　＿＿＿＿＿＿＿＿＿＿＿＿＿＿＿？
3. 疼痛反复出现。　　　＿＿＿＿＿＿＿＿＿＿＿＿＿＿＿？
4. 病人的疼痛不严重。　＿＿＿＿＿＿＿＿＿＿＿＿＿＿＿？

语法点 2 Grammar Point 2

提问的方法：用"什么、哪里、多少、多"提问　Way of asking questions: questions with "什么，哪里，多少，多"

用疑问代词提问的疑问句是特殊疑问句，要求对方有针对性地回答，如"什么"（问事物）；"哪里"（问地点）；"多少"（问数量）；"多+形容词"（问数量或程度）等。A question with an interrogative pronoun is a special question, which requires the other party to give a specific answer. For example: "什么" (asking about things), "哪里" (asking about the location), "多少" (asking about the quantity), "多 + adj" (asking about the quantity or degree), etc.

73

例句：
1. Téngtòng de yòuyīn shì shénme?
   疼痛的诱因是什么？ What are the causes of the pain?

2. Téngtòng de zhèngzhuàng yǒu duōjiǔ?
   疼痛的 症状 有多久？ How long have the symptoms of pain appeared?

3. Bìngrén de bìngqíng duō yánzhòng?
   病人的病情 多 严重？ How serious is the patient's condition?

语法练习 2 Grammar Exercise 2

用"什么""多+严重/久"对画线词语提问。Ask questions about underlined words using "什么" and "多+严重/久".

1. 疼痛的诱因是<u>脊柱损伤</u>。
   _____

2. 病人的病情为<u>一级</u>。
   _____

3. 疼痛的时间为<u>一天</u>（tiān, day）。
   _____

4. 救护车<u>15分钟</u>内赶到病人家里。
   _____

汉字书写 Writing Chinese Characters

gōng
工 工 工
工 工 工 工 工

第 8 课 | 收集信息

tǔ 土 土 土
土 土 土 土 土

lǐ 里 里 里 里 里 里 里
里 里 里 里 里

lǐ 理 理 理 理 理 理 理 理 理 理 理
理 理 理 理 理

职业拓展 Career Insight

History of Emergency Medicine Development in China

In China, modern emergency medicine has evolved from its early stages of simplicity to a more sophisticated and independent discipline. The development timeline includes several key milestones:

In the early 1970s, cardiac care units and comprehensive care units were established. In 1981, the *Chinese Journal of Critical Care Medicine* was founded. In 1983, the first emergency department was set up at Peking Union Medical College Hospital. In 1985, the first large-scale monograph on emergency medicine, *Emergency Clinical Practice*, was published. In the same year, the first Master of Emergency Medicine Postgraduate Training Center was established. In 1986, the emergency medical law of China was passed. In 1987, the Emergency Medicine Branch of the Chinese Medical Association was officially established.

These milestones mark the formal establishment of emergency medicine as a distinct and independent discipline in China.

小结 Summary

词语 Words

朗读词语。Read the words aloud.

诱因	症状	部位
放射痛	严重	反复

语法 Grammar

朗读句子。Read the sentences aloud.

1. 有放射痛吗？
2. 症状反复出现吗？
3. 症状有多久？
4. 疼痛程度多严重？

课文理解 Text Comprehension

根据表格说明怎样用PQRST法收集病人信息。Explain how to use PQRST method to collect patients' information according to the table.

PQRST 法				
P	Q	R	S 0—10	T
疼痛的诱因是什么？	症状的性质是什么？	有无放射痛？部位在哪里？	疼痛程度是多少？	症状有多久？反复出现吗？

第9课 初级评估
Lesson 9　Primary Assessment
（Chūjí pínggū）

复习　Revision

选词填空。Fill in the blanks with the correct words.

1. P：疼痛的_____。
2. Q：症状的_____。
3. R：有无_____。
4. S：疼痛的_____。

A 程度　　　B 放射痛
C 性质　　　D 诱因

热身　Warming Up

看图选词。Look at the pictures and choose the correct words.

A 温度 temperature（wēndù）　　B 脉搏 pulse（màibó）
C 皮肤 skin（pífū）　　D 毛细血管 capillary（máoxì-xuèguǎn）

77

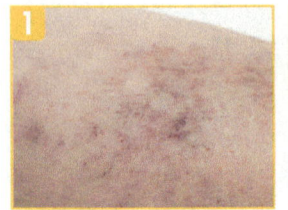

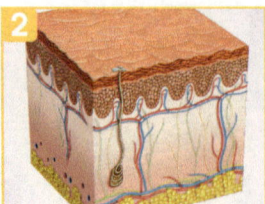

学习生词　Words and Expressions　9-1

1	初级	chūjí	*adj.*	primary
2	能	néng	*v.*	can
3	早期	zǎoqī	*n.*	early stage
4	发现	fāxiàn	*v.*	detect
5	威胁	wēixié	*v.*	threaten
6	状况	zhuàngkuàng	*n.*	situation
7	判断	pànduàn	*v.*	determine
8	是否	shìfǒu	*adv.*	whether
9	通畅	tōngchàng	*adj.*	unobstructed
10	频率	pínlǜ	*n.*	frequency
11	深度	shēndù	*n.*	depth
12	正常	zhèngcháng	*adj.*	normal
13	皮肤	pífū	*n.*	skin
14	温度	wēndù	*n.*	temperature
15	脉搏	màibó	*n.*	pulse

第 9 课 | 初级评估

| 16 | 毛细血管 | máoxì-xuèguǎn | *n.* | capillary |

词语练习 Words Exercises

1. 看图说词。Look at the pictures and say the words.

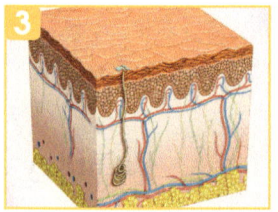

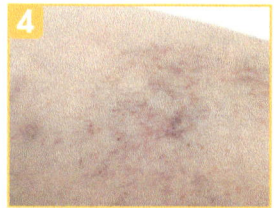

2. 朗读短语。Read the phrases aloud.

威胁生命　　气道通畅　　呼吸正常　　皮肤颜色

学习课文 Text 🎧 9-2

初级评估
Chūjí pínggū

Chūjí pínggū néng zài zǎoqī fāxiàn wēixié shēngmìng de zhuàngkuàng,
初级评估能在早期发现威胁生命的状况，
kěyǐ shǐyòng fǎ.
可以使用 ABCD 法。

　　　Pànduàn qìdào shìfǒu tōngchàng.
A：判断气道是否通畅。

　　　Pínggū hūxī de pínlǜ, shēndù děng shìfǒu zhèngcháng.
B：评估呼吸的频率、深度等是否正常。

79

C：评估皮肤颜色、温度、脉搏和毛细血管的状况是否正常。

D：判断病人的意识状况。

Primary Assessment

Primary assessment can detect life-threatening situations in early stage. The ABCD method can be used.

A: Determine if the airway is unobstructed.

B: Assess whether the frequency, depth, and other aspects of breathing are normal.

C: Assess whether the skin color, temperature, pulse, and the condition of capillaries are normal.

D: Assess the patient's level of consciousness.

课文练习 Text Exercises

1. 判断正误。True or false.

① 初级评估可以在早期发现威胁生命的状况。

② ABCD 法是初级评估的方法。

③ B 是评估病人气道是否通畅。

④ D 是评估病人的意识状况。

2. 选词填空。Fill in the blanks with the correct words.

> A 脉搏　　　　B 意识　　　　C 气道　　　　D 呼吸

1. A：判断_____是否通畅。
2. B：评估_____的频率、深度等是否正常。
3. C：评估皮肤颜色、温度、_____和毛细血管的状况是否正常。
4. D：判断病人的_____状况。

学习语法 Grammar

语法点 1 Grammar Point 1

能愿动词：能　Modal verb: 能

能愿动词"能"表示有能力或有可能，后面接动词。否定形式是"不能"。

The modal verb "能" indicates having the ability or possibility. It is followed by a verb. The negative form is "不能".

例句：
1. 初级评估能在早期发现威胁生命的状况。Primary assessment can detect life-threatening situations in early stage.
2. 救护车能尽快赶到病人家里吗？Can the ambulance arrive at the patient's home as soon as possible?
3. 不能移动脊柱损伤的病人。Patients with spinal injuries cannot be moved.

语法练习 1　Grammar Exercise 1

按照正确的语序连词成句。Make sentences in correct orders with the given words or phrases.

1 ①在早期发现　②初级评估　③能　④威胁生命的状况

_____

2 ①尽快赶到　②救护车　③能　④病人家里

_____

3 ①能　②不　③脊柱损伤病人　④移动

_____

4 ①吸痰、吸氧等急救措施　②病人的呼吸和循环功能　③能　④维持

_____

语法点 2　Grammar Point 2

副词：是否　Adverb: 是否

"否"的意思是"不是"。副词"是否"用于疑问句中，要求对方作出肯定或否定的回答。

The meaning of "否" is "不是" (not). The adverb "是否" is used in an interrogative sentence, requiring the other party to give an affirmative or negative answer.

例句：

1 病人的气道是否 通畅？　Is the patient's airway unobstructed?
　　Bìngrén de qìdào shìfǒu tōngchàng?

2 病人呼吸的频率、深度等是否 正常？　Are the patient's breathing frequency, depth, and other aspects normal?
　　Bìngrén hūxī de pínlǜ, shēndù děng shìfǒu zhèngcháng?

3 Bìngrén shìfǒu yǒu yìshi?
病人是否有意识？ Is the patient conscious?

语法练习 2 Grammar Exercise 2

用"是否"改写句子。Rewrite the sentences with "是否".

1. 病人的气道通畅吗？ _____
2. 病人的呼吸频率正常吗？ _____
3. 病人有意识吗？ _____
4. 你有放射痛吗？ _____

汉字书写 Writing Chinese Characters

dà 大 大 大 大
大 大 大 大 大

xiǎo 小 小 小
小 小 小 小 小

duō 多 多 多 多 多 多
多 多 多 多 多

shǎo 少 少 少 少
少 少 少 少 少

文化拓展 Culture Insight

Hua Tuo

Hua Tuo, born around 145 AD, was one of the pioneers of ancient Chinese medical sports. He created an exercise system called "Five Animals Play," based on the principle that "running water is never stale, and a door hinge never gets worm-eaten." This form of gymnastics imitates the movements and postures of five animals: the tiger, deer, bear, ape, and bird.

By mimicking these animals, practitioners can stretch and strengthen the joints, back, waist, and limbs. "Five Animals Play" is known to help improve physical strength, and those who are ill can also speed up their recovery through these exercises. Even elderly individuals who practice the "Five Animals Play" can maintain energy and vitality, feeling more radiant and physically invigorated.

小结 Summary

词语 Words

朗读词语。Read the words aloud.

通畅	频率	皮肤
温度	脉搏	毛细血管

语法 Grammar

朗读句子。Read the sentences aloud.

1. 初级评估能在早期发现威胁生命的状况。
2. 不能移动脊柱损伤的病人。
3. 判断气道是否通畅。
4. 评估皮肤颜色是否正常。

课文理解 Text Comprehension

填表，说明用于初级评估的 ABCD 法。Fill in the table, and explain the ABCD method for primary assessment.

初级评估 ABCD 法	
目的（mùdì, objective）	
A	气道： ☐有通畅 ☐不通畅
B	呼吸的频率和深度：☐有正常 ☐不正常
C	皮肤颜色、温度、脉搏和毛细血管： ☐正常 ☐不正常
D	意识： ☐有 ☐没有

第10课 Lesson 10

次级评估（问诊）
Cìjí pínggū (wènzhěn)
Secondary Assessment (Consultation)

复习 Revision

选词填空。Fill in the blanks with the correct words.

1. 初级评估能在早期发现_____生命的状况。
2. 判断_____是否正常。
3. 评估呼吸的_____和深度等是否正常。
4. 判断病人的_____状况。

A 频率　B 威胁
C 意识　D 气道

热身 Warming Up

看图选词。Look at the pictures and choose the correct words.

A 过敏 (guòmǐn) be allergic to　　B 食物 (shíwù) food
C 手术 (shǒushù) surgery　　D 外伤 (wàishāng) external injury

86

第 10 课 | 次级评估（问诊）

学习生词 Words and Expressions 🎧 10-1

1	次级	cìjí	*a.*	secondary
2	问诊	wènzhěn	*v.*	consult
3	获得	huòdé	*v.*	obtain
4	病史	bìngshǐ	*n,*	medical history
5	舒服	shūfu	*adj.*	well
6	食物	shíwù	*n.*	food
7	过敏	guòmǐn	*v.*	be allergic to
8	现在	xiànzài	*n.*	now
9	用药	yòngyào		medication
10	情况	qíngkuàng	*n.*	situation

87

11	以前	yǐqián	n.	before
12	过	guò	aux.	(used after a verb to indicate the completion of an action)
13	这种	zhè zhǒng		this kind of
14	做	zuò	v.	do
15	手术	shǒushù	n.	surgery
16	家族	jiāzú	n.	family
17	上次	shàngcì	n.	last time
18	就餐	jiùcān	v.	have a meal
19	现病史	xiànbìngshǐ	n.	current medical history
20	外伤史	wàishāngshǐ	n.	traumatic history

词语练习 Words Exercises

1. 看图说词。 Look at the pictures and say the words.

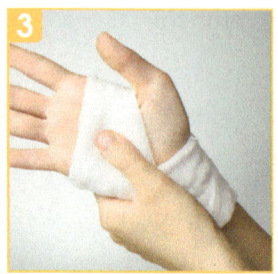

第 10 课 | 次级评估（问诊）

2. 朗读短语。Read the phrases aloud.

- 病史
- 家族病史
- 现病史
- 外伤史
- 用药情况
- 这种情况
- 就餐情况
- 对什么食物过敏
- 对什么药物过敏

学习课文 Text 🎧 10-2

次级评估（问诊）
Cìjí pínggū (wènzhěn)

Shǐyòng fǎ kěyǐ huòdé bìngrén de bìngshǐ xìnxī.
使用 SAMPLE 法可以获得病人的病史信息。

S：您不舒服吗？
Nín bù shūfu ma?

A：您对什么药物、食物过敏？
Nín duì shénme yàowù、shíwù guòmǐn?

M：现在的用药情况？
Xiànzài de yòngyào qíngkuàng?

P：以前有过这种情况吗？做过手术吗？有没有家族病史？
Yǐqián yǒuguò zhè zhǒng qíngkuàng ma? Zuòguò shǒushù ma? Yǒu méiyǒu jiāzú bìngshǐ?

L：上次就餐情况？
Shàngcì jiùcān qíngkuàng?

E：现病史？外伤史？
Xiànbìngshǐ? Wàishāngshǐ?

Secondary Assessment (Consultation)

The SAMPLE method can be used to obtain the patient's medical history information.

S: Are you feeling unwell?

A: What medicine or food are you allergic to?

M: What is the current medication situation?

P: Have you ever had this situation before? Have you ever had any surgery? Do you have a family medical history?

L: What is the situation of last meal?

E: What is the current medical history? What is the traumatic history?

课文练习 Text Exercises

1. 判断正误。True or false.

① 使用 SAMPLE 法可以获得病人的病史信息。

② A 是问病人对什么过敏。

③ P 是问用药情况。

④ E 是问以前是否有过这种病。

2. 选词填空。Fill in the blanks with the correct words.

① S：您不_____吗?

　A 舒服　　　B 过敏　　　C 食物

② A：您对什么食物、药物_____?

　A 舒服　　　B 过敏　　　C 获得

3 P：做过_____吗？

A 手术　　　　B 外伤　　　　C 情况

4 L：上次_____情况？

A 食物　　　　B 就餐　　　　C 手术

学习语法 Grammar

语法点 1　Grammar Point 1

时态助词：过　　Aspectual particle: 过

助词"过"放在动词后面，表示行为或变化曾经发生。
The particle "过" is used after a verb to indicate that the certain behavior or change has happened before.

例句：

1 你以前有过这种情况吗？ Have you ever had this situation before?

Nǐ yǐqián yǒuguò zhè zhǒng qíngkuàng ma?

2 你做过手术吗？ Have you ever had any surgery?

Nǐ zuòguò shǒushù ma?

3 你以前有过这种病吗？ Have you ever had this disease before?

Nǐ yǐqián yǒuguò zhè zhǒng bìng ma?

语法练习 1　Grammar Exercise 1

把"过"放在句中合适的位置。Put "过" in the right place in the sentence.

1 他____以前____做____手术。

2 你____以前____有____这种病____吗？

③ 你____有____外伤____吗____？

④ 你____评估____病人的____病情____吗？

语法点 2 Grammar Point 2

提问的方法：用正反疑问形式提问　Way of asking questions: the question with the affirmative and negative forms together

用谓语的肯定形式和否定形式并列起来提问是正反疑问句，要求对方作出肯定或否定的回答。

A question in which the affirmative and negative forms of the predicate are juxtaposed is called an affirmative-negative question, which requires the other party to provide a positive or negative answer.

例句：
① Nǐ yǒu méiyǒu jiāzú bìngshǐ?
你有没有家族病史？　Do you have a family medical history?

② Nín shì bú shì bù shūfu?
您是不是不舒服？　Are you feeling unwell?

③ Nǐ zuò méi zuòguò shǒushù?
你做没做过手术？　Have you ever had any surgery?

语法练习 2 Grammar Exercise 2

把陈述句改成正反疑问句。Change the declarative sentences into affirmative-negative question sentences.

① 我没有家族病史。　_____

② 我不舒服。　_____

③ 我以前做过手术。　_____

④ 病人有外伤史。　_____

第 10 课 | 次级评估（问诊）

汉字书写 Writing Chinese Characters

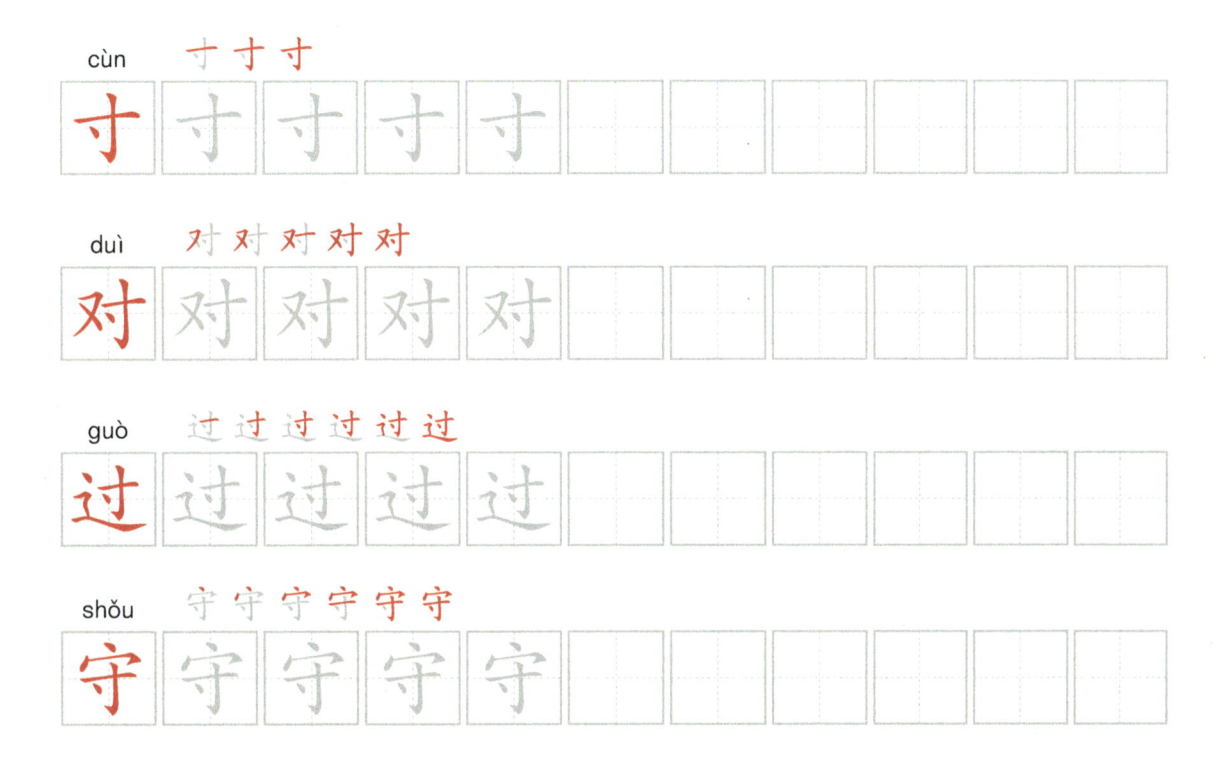

cùn
寸 寸 寸 寸
寸 寸 寸 寸 寸

duì
对 对 对 对 对
对 对 对 对 对

guò
过 过 过 过 过 过
过 过 过 过 过

shǒu
守 守 守 守 守 守
守 守 守 守 守

职业拓展 Career Insight

China Clinical Key Specialty (Emergency Department) Construction Project

The National Health Commission has issued the "14th Five-Year Plan for National Clinical Specialized Capacity Building". The plan proposes to implement the "Ten Million Project" for clinical key specialties during the 14th Five-Year Plan period. At the national level, cumulative support will be provided for the construction of no less than 750 national clinical key

93

specialty construction projects across the country, with appropriate distribution among different provinces based on their specific medical resource situations. Through project construction, a grid-based clinical specialized service system will be formed.

小结 Summary

词语 Words

朗读词语。Read the words aloud.

手术	过敏	外伤
用药	不舒服	做手术

语法 Grammar

朗读句子。Read the sentences aloud.

1. 以前有过这种情况吗？
2. 做过手术吗？
3. 有没有家族病史？
4. 您是不是不舒服？

课文理解 Text Comprehension

填表，说明用于次级评估（问诊）的 SAMPLE 法。Fill in the table, and explain the SAMPLE method for secondary assessment (consultation).

	用 SAMPLE 法问病史
目的	
S	☐舒服　　☐不舒服
A	☐过敏　　☐不过敏　　对_____过敏
M	☐正常　　☐不正常
P	以前：☐有过　　☐没有过 手术：☐做过　　☐没做过 家族病史：☐有过　　☐没有过
L	上次就餐：☐正常　　☐不正常
E	现病史：_____ 外伤史：_____

第11课 Lesson 11

次级评估（生命体征）
Secondary Assessment (Vital Signs)

复习 Revision

选择正确的答案。Choose the correct answers.

| A 用药情况 | B 过敏 | C 做过手术等 |
| D 不舒服 | E 现病史和外伤史 | F 就餐情况 |

用 SAMPLE 法问病史：

S: _____   A: _____   M: _____

P: _____   L: _____   E: _____

第 11 课 | 次级评估（生命体征）

热身 Warming Up

看图选词。Look at the pictures and choose the correct words.

A 体重 tǐzhòng weight　　B 监测 jiāncè monitor　　C 体温 tǐwēn body temperature

D 舒张压／收缩压 shūzhāngyā/shōusuōyā diastolic pressure/systolic pressure

| 1 | 2 | 3 | 4 |

学习生词 Words and Expressions　11-1

1	包括	bāokuò	v.	include
2	体温	tǐwēn	n.	body temperature
3	血压	xuèyā	n.	blood pressure
4	血氧饱和度	xuèyǎng bǎohédù	n.	blood oxygen saturation
5	体重	tǐzhòng	n.	weight
6	因为	yīnwèi	conj.	because
7	连续	liánxù	v.	in succession
8	发展	fāzhǎn	v.	develop

97

9	过程	guòchéng	n.	process
10	所以	suǒyǐ	*conj.*	so
11	监测	jiāncè	*v.*	monitor
12	范围	fànwéi	*n.*	range
13	每	měi	*pron.*	every
14	次	cì	*measure word*	time
15	收缩压	shōusuōyā	*n.*	systolic pressure
16	舒张压	shūzhāngyā	*n.*	diastolic pressure

词语练习 Words Exercises

1. 看图说词。 Look at the pictures and say the words.

2. 朗读短语。 Read the phrases aloud.

① 生命体征：体温　　脉搏　　呼吸　　血压　　血氧饱和度　　体重

② 体温：36°C—37°C

③ 脉搏：60—100 次/分钟

④ 呼吸频率：16—20 次/分钟

⑤ 收缩压：90—139mmHg

⑥ 舒张压：60—89mmHg

注释 Notes:

°C 读作摄氏度（shèshìdù）。mmHg 读作毫米汞柱（háomǐ-gǒngzhù）。

°C is pronounced as "shèshìdù". mmHg is pronounced as "háomǐ-gǒngzhù".

学习课文 Text 11-2

次级评估（生命体征）
Cìjí pínggū (shēngmìng tǐzhēng)

生命体征包括体温、脉搏、呼吸、血压、血氧饱和度和体重。因为病情是一个连续发展的过程，所以要连续监测病人的生命体征。正常范围内的体温为 36 — 37°C；脉搏为每分钟 60 — 100 次；呼吸频率为每分钟 16 — 20 次；收缩压为 90 — 139 mmHg，舒张压为 60 — 89 mmHg。

Secondary Assessment (Vital Signs)

Vital signs include body temperature, pulse, respiration, blood pressure, blood oxygen saturation, and weight. Because the disease condition is a contunuously developing process, it is necessary to continuously monitor the patient's vital signs. The normal range for the body temperature is 36–37 ℃; for the pulse is 60–100 times per minute; for the respiratory rate is 16–20 times per minute; for the systolic blood pressure is 90–139mmHg, and for the diastolic blood pressure is 60–89mmHg.

课文练习 Text Exercises

1. 判断正误。True or false.

① 意识是生命体征。

② 病情是一个连续发展的过程。

③ 37℃ 是正常体温。

④ 收缩压的正常范围是 60—89mmHg。

2. 选词填空。Fill in the blanks with the correct words.

A 频率	B 连续	C 体征	D 每

① 病情是一个_____发展的过程。

2 要连续监测病人的生命_____。

3 脉搏的正常范围为_____分钟 60—100 次。

4 呼吸_____的正常范围是每分钟 16—20 次。

学习语法 Grammar

语法点 1 Grammar Point 1

因果复句：因为……所以……　Causative complex sentence: 因为 ... 所以 ...

关联词语"因为""所以"连接因果复句，前一分句是原因，后一分句是推论或结果。两个关联词可以搭配使用，也可以只用一个。

The correlatives "因为" and "所以" can be used to connect a causative complex sentence, in which the preceding clause is the cause and the following clause is the inference or result. The two correlatives can be used both or singly.

例句：

1 因为病情是一个连续发展的过程，所以要连续监测病人的生命体征。Because the disease condition is a continuously developing process, it is necessary to continuously monitor the patient's vital signs.

2 因为病人随时有生命危险，要马上抢救。Because the patient's life is at risk at any time, immediate rescue is necessary.

3 病人脊柱损伤，所以不要移动。The patient has a spinal injury, so do not move him.

语法练习 1 Grammar Exercise 1

用"因为……所以……"完成句子。Complete the sentences with "因为...所以...".

1 病人脊柱损伤　　不要移动

_____

2 病人随时有生命危险　　要马上抢救

_____

3 病情不急　　病人分诊为四级

_____

4 病情是一个连续发展的过程　　要连续监测病人的生命体征

_____

语法点 2 Grammar Point 2

时间词　Time words

表示时间的词有"年、月、日、小时、分钟、秒"等。时间词也可以充当量词。
Time words include 年 (nián, year), 月 (yuè, month), 日 (rì, day), 小时 (xiǎoshí, hour), 分钟 (fēnzhōng, minute), 秒 (miǎo, second), etc. Time words can be also used as measure words.

例句：
1 脉搏频率为每分钟 60 — 100 次。
Màibó pínlǜ wéi měi fēnzhōng liùshí zhì yìbǎi cì.
The pulse rate is 60–100 times per minute.

2 救护车 15 分钟内赶到。
Jiùhùchē shíwǔ fēnzhōng nèi gǎndào.
The ambulance will arrive within 15 minutes.

3 呼吸频率为每分钟 60 — 20 次。
Hūxī pínlǜ wéi měi fēnzhōng liùshí zhì èrshí cì.
The respiratory rate is 16–20 times per minute.

第 11 课 | 次级评估（生命体征）

语法练习 2 Grammar Exercise 2

选择正确的答案。Choose the correct answers.

A 10 分钟　B 30 分钟　C 16—20 次 / 分钟　D 60—100 次 / 分钟

1. 呼吸频率的正常范围为_____。
2. 脉搏频率的正常范围为_____。
3. 活动性出血要马上监护，在_____内治疗。
4. 腹痛要在_____内治疗。

汉字书写 Writing Chinese Characters

shàng 上 上 上 上

xià 下 下 下 下

zuǒ 左 左 左 左 左

yòu 右 右 右 右 右

103

文化拓展 Culture Insight

Zhang Zhongjing and Dumplings

The dumplings, are a beloved traditional Chinese delicacy. It is believed that the renowned "medical sage" Zhang Zhongjing invented them during the late Eastern Han Dynasty (25–220 AD). During this period, disasters and diseases were widespread, and many people suffered from illness. While passing by the Baihe River in his hometown, Zhang Zhongjing observed the dire conditions of the poor, many of whom had frozen and decayed ears due to the harsh cold. Moved by their plight, he decided to help them.

Zhang Zhongjing boiled lamb, chili peppers, and several herbs known for their ability to dispel cold, and wrapped the mixture in dough to form shapes resembling ears. He then cooked the "ear-shaped" dumplings and distributed them to the sick. After consuming this special remedy, the patients' fever subsided, their blood circulated freely, and their frozen ears were healed.

Zhang Zhongjing continued his medicinal work until Chinese New Year's Eve. On the first day of the Chinese New Year, people not only celebrated the new year but also the recovery of their damaged ears. They began preparing this special "ear-shaped" food, which eventually became known as dumplings.

小结 Summary

词语 Words

朗读词语。Read the words aloud.

体征	体重	体温	血氧饱和度
监测	血压	收缩压	舒张压

语法 Grammar

朗读句子。Read the sentences aloud.

1. 因为病情是一个连续发展的过程，所以要连续监测病人的生命体征。
2. 因为病人的体温不正常，所以我们要连续监测。
3. 脉搏的正常范围为每分钟60—100次。
4. 呼吸频率的正常范围为每分钟16—20次。

课文理解 Text Comprehension

填空，说明怎样评估病人的生命体征。Fill in the blanks and explain how to evaluate the patient's vital signs.

生命体征正常的范围：

体温：_____°C　　　　　　　脉搏：_____次/分钟

呼吸频率：_____次/分钟

血压：收缩压：_____mmHg；舒张压：_____mmHg

第12课 Lesson 12

次级评估（身体部位）
Cìjí pínggū (shēntǐ bùwèi)
Secondary Assessment (Body Parts)

复习 Revision

朗读句子。 Read the sentences aloud.

1. 体温、脉搏、呼吸等都是生命体征。
2. 病情是一个连续发展的过程。
3. 要连续监测病人的生命体征。
4. 收缩压的正常范围是 90—139mmHg，舒张压是 60—89mmHg。

第 12 课 | 次级评估（身体部位）

热身 Warming Up

看图，学说人体部位的名称。Look at the picture and learn to say the names of human body parts.

A 头部 (tóubù) head	B 颈部 (jǐngbù) neck	C 胸部 (xiōngbù) chest
D 腹部 (fùbù) abdomen	E 背部 (bèibù) back	F 四肢 (sìzhī) limb
G 眼（眼睛）(yǎn/yǎnjing) eye	H 耳（耳朵）(ěr/ěrduo) ear	I 鼻（鼻子）(bí/bízi) nose

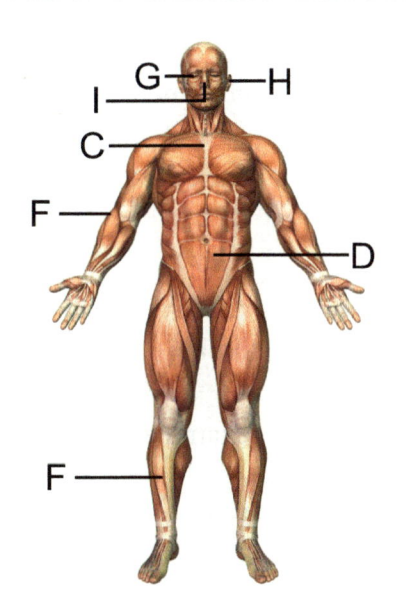

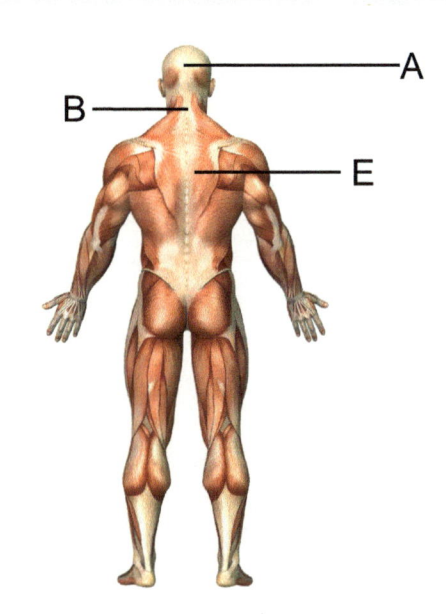

学习生词 Words and Expressions 🎧 12-1

1	身体	shēntǐ	n.	body
2	重症	zhòngzhèng	n.	critical illness

107

3	都	dōu	*adv.*	all
4	需要	xūyào	*v.*	need
5	所有	suǒyǒu	*adj.*	all
6	重点	zhòngdiǎn	*n.*	key
7	头	tóu	*n.*	head
8	颈	jǐng	*n.*	neck
9	胸	xiōng	*n.*	chest
10	腹	fù	*n.*	abdomen
11	背	bèi	*n.*	back
12	部	bù	*suffix*	part
13	四肢	sìzhī	*n.*	limbs
14	检查	jiǎnchá	*v.*	examine
15	眼（眼睛）	yǎn (yǎnjīng)	*n.*	eye
16	耳（耳朵）	ěr (ěrduo)	*n.*	ear
17	鼻（鼻子）	bí (bízi)	*n.*	nose
18	神经系统	shénjīng xìtǒng		nervous system
19	昏迷	hūnmí	*v.*	be in a coma
20	评分	píngfēn	*n.*	score

第 12 课 | 次级评估（身体部位）

> 词语练习　Words Exercises

1. 在图上指出下面几个人体部位。Point out the following body parts on the picture.

A 胸部　　B 背部　　C 腹部　　D 四肢　　E 眼　　F 鼻

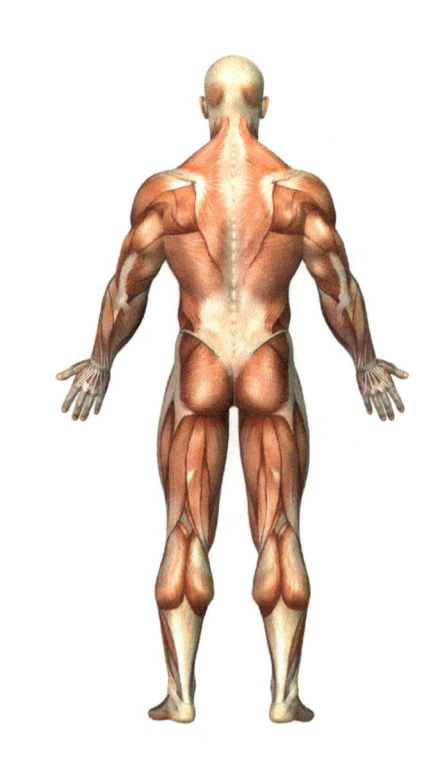

2. 朗读短语。Read the phrases aloud.

| 重症病人 | 轻症病人 | 昏迷的病人 |

评估所有身体部位

| 评估重点部位 | 检查外伤 | 检查神经系统 |

109

学习课文　Text　🎧 12-2

次级评估（身体部位）

医生需要评估的身体部位包括：头部、颈部、胸部、腹部、背部和四肢。对于重症病人，所有的身体部位都需要评估。对于轻症病人，医生可以评估重点部位。例如：评估头部需要检查外伤、眼、耳、鼻和神经系统。对昏迷病人可以使用 GCS 评分法。

Secondary Assessment (Body Parts)

The body parts that need to be assessed include: head, neck, chest, abdomen, back, and limbs. For critically ill patients, all body parts of the patient need to be assessed. For mild patients, doctors can assess key parts. For example, the head needs to be examined for trauma, eyes, ears, nose, and nervous system. GCS scoring method can be used for comatose patients.

第 12 课 | 次级评估（身体部位）

课文练习 Text Exercises

1. 判断正误。True or false.

1. 对于重症病人，医生需要评估重点部位。
2. 对于轻症病人，医生可以评估所有的身体部位。
3. 头部检查的部位包括神经系统。
4. 对昏迷病人可以使用 GCS 评分法。

2. 根据课文内容回答问题。Answer the questions according to the text.

1. 对于重症病人，需要评估什么部位？

   _____

2. 对于轻症病人，需要评估什么部位？

   _____

3. 医生评估的部位包括什么？

   _____

4. 对昏迷病人，使用什么评估方法？

   _____

学习语法 Grammar

语法点 1 Grammar Point 1

能愿动词：需要　Modal verb: 需要

能愿动词"需要"放在动词前面，表示必须、应该。
The modal verb "需要" is used before the verb to indicate the meaning of "must" and "should".

111

例句：

1. 　Duìyú zhòngzhèng bìngrén, yīshēng xūyào pínggū bìngrén suǒyǒu de shēntǐ bùwèi.
对于 重症 病人，医生 需要 评估 病人 所有 的 身体 部位。 For critically ill patients, doctors need to assess all body parts of the patient.

2. 　Yīshēng xūyào pínggū bìngrén de tóubù, jǐngbù děng bùwèi.
医生 需要 评估 病人 的 头部、颈部 等 部位。 Doctors need to assess the patient's head, neck, and other parts.

3. 　Tóubù xūyào jiǎnchá wàishāng, yǎn děng.
头部 需要 检查 外伤、眼 等。 The head needs to be examined for trauma, eyes, etc.

语法练习 1　Grammar Exercise 1

选择正确的答案。Choose the correct answers.

A 所有身体部位　　　　B 外伤、眼等
C 头、颈、胸等部位　　D 连续监测

1. 对于重症病人，医生需要评估_____。
2. 对于轻症病人，医生需要评估_____。
3. 评估头部，需要检查_____。
4. 病人的生命体征需要_____。

语法点 2　Grammar Point 2

名词：部　Noun: 部

"N＋部"可以构成表示身体部位的名词。
"N＋部" can form the nouns that represent body parts.

第 12 课 | 次级评估（身体部位）

tóubù	jǐngbù	xiōngbù	fùbù	bèibù
头部	颈部	胸部	腹部	背部
head	neck	chest	abdomen	back

语法练习 2 Grammar Exercise 2

看图片，说出箭头指向的身体部位名称。Look at the picture and say the names of the body parts that the arrows point to.

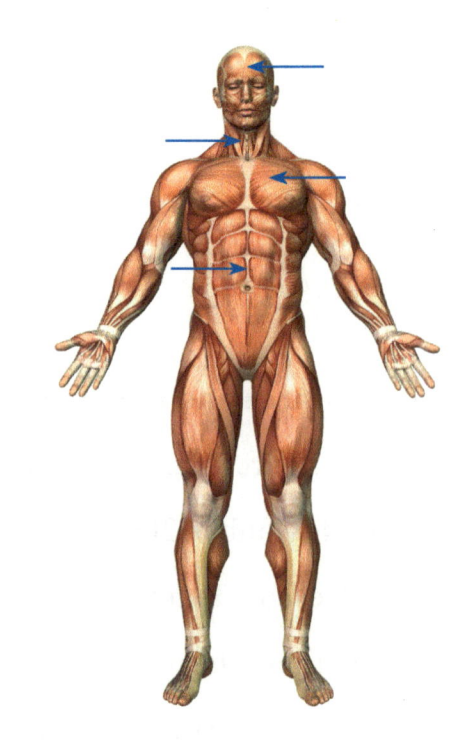

汉字书写 Writing Chinese Characters

kǒu

口 口 口

口 口 口 口 口

113

zhōng 中 中 中 中
中 中 中 中 中

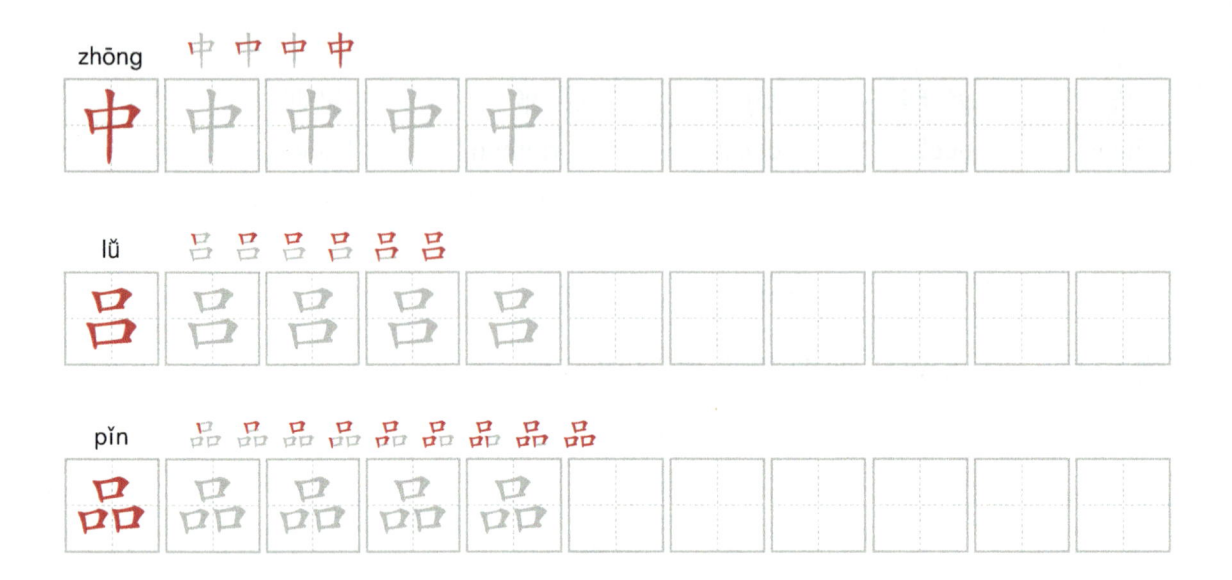

lǚ 吕 吕 吕 吕 吕 吕
吕 吕 吕 吕 吕

pǐn 品 品 品 品 品 品 品 品 品
品 品 品 品 品

职业拓展 Career Insight

China International Search and Rescue Team (CISAR)

The China International Search and Rescue Team (CISAR) was established in April 2001. In November 2009, CISAR passed the United Nations International Heavy Rescue Team Grading Assessment, earning certification as the 12th international heavy rescue team in the world and the second in Asia. Since its inception, CISAR has participated in international rescue operations in countries such as Algeria, Iran, Indonesia, Pakistan, Haiti, New Zealand, and Japan.

第 12 课 | 次级评估（身体部位）

小结 Summary

词语 Words

朗读词语。Read the words aloud.

| 重症 | 四肢 | 头部 |
| 昏迷 | 眼 | 神经系统 |

语法 Grammar

朗读句子。Read the sentences aloud.

1. 重症病人所有的身体部位都需要评估。
2. 头部评估需要检查外伤等。
3. 医生评估的身体部位包括头部、颈部等。
4. 评估头部需要检查外伤和神经系统等。

课文理解 Text Comprehension

根据下表，说明怎样评估病人的身体部位。Explain how to assess the patient's body parts according to the table below.

评估身体部位
- 重症病人 —— 所有部位 —— 头部 —— 外伤 / 眼、耳、鼻 / 神经系统
- 轻症病人 —— 重点部位 —— 颈部 / 胸部 / 腹部 / 背部 / 四肢
- 昏迷病人 —— GCS 评分法

115

第13课 Lesson 13

测量体温、脉搏和呼吸
Cèliáng tǐwēn, màibó hé hūxī

Measuring Body Temperature, Pulse, and Respiration

复习 Revision

选择正确的答案。Choose the correct answers.

1. 对于重症病人，医生需要评估病人所有的_____部位。

   A 头部　　　　　　B 身体　　　　　　C 颈部

2. 对于_____病人，医生可以评估重点部位。

   A 轻症　　　　　　B 昏迷　　　　　　C 重症

3. 医生评估的身体部位包括：_____、颈部、胸部、腹部、背部和四肢。

   A 神经系统　　　　B 鼻子　　　　　　C 头部

4. 评估头部需要检查外伤、_____、耳、鼻和神经系统。

   A 腹部　　　　　　B 眼　　　　　　　C 背部

116

第 13 课 | 测量体温、脉搏和呼吸

热身 Warming Up

看图选词。Look at the pictures and choose the correct words.

A 测量 (cèliáng) measure
B 体温计 (tǐwēnjì) thermometer
C 手指肚 (shǒuzhǐdù) finger pads
D 记录 (jìlù) record

| 1 | 2 | 3 | 4 |

学习生词 Words and Expressions 🎧 13-1

1	测量	cèliáng	v.	measure
2	前	qián	n.	before
3	休息	xiūxi	v.	rest
4	把	bǎ	prep.	(used to advance the object of a verb to the position before it)
5	体温计	tǐwēnjì	n.	thermometer
6	甩	shuǎi	v.	swing

117

7	到	dào	v.	(used as a verb complement to indicate the result of an action)
8	以下	yǐxià	n.	below
9	手指肚	shǒuzhǐdù	n.	finger pad
10	按	àn	v.	press
11	桡动脉	ráodòngmài	n.	radial artery
12	秒	miǎo	n.	second
13	起伏	qǐfú	v.	fluctuate
14	记录	jìlù	v.	record
15	结果	jiéguǒ	n.	result

词语练习 Words Exercises

1. 看图说词。 Look at the pictures and say the words.

2. 朗读短语。 Read the phrases aloud.

测量体温　　测量脉搏　　测量呼吸

休息 30 分钟　　按桡动脉 30 秒　　记录结果

学习课文 Text 🎧 13-2

测量体温、脉搏和呼吸

测量体温、脉搏和呼吸前，病人要休息 30 分钟。

1. 测体温：把体温计的温度甩到 35°C 以下，测量体温，5 分钟。

2. 测脉搏：把三个手指肚按在病人的桡动脉上，30 秒。

3. 测呼吸：观察病人胸部的起伏，30 秒。

4. 记录结果。

Measure Body Temperature, Pulse, and Respiration

Before measuring body temperature, pulse, and respiration, patients should rest for 30 minutes.

1. Measure body temperature: Swing the thermometer to

make its temperature drop below 35°C and measure the patient's body temperature for 5 minutes.

2. Measure pulse: Press three finger pads on the patient's radial artery for 30 seconds.

3. Measure respiration: Observe the fluctuation of the patient's chest for 30 seconds.

4. Record the results.

课文练习 Text Exercises

1. 判断正误。True or false.

1 测量体温前，病人要休息。

2 测量体温前，温度计的温度要在35°C以下。

3 测量体温需要5分钟。

4 护士测呼吸要把手指肚要按在病人的桡动脉上。

2. 选词填空。Fill in the blanks with the correct answers.

1 测量体温、脉搏、呼吸前，病人要_____30分钟。

　　A 休息　　　　B 观察　　　　C 检查

2 测量体温前体温计的温度应该甩到35°C_____。

　　A 中间　　　　B 前　　　　　C 以下

3 手指肚按在桡动脉上30_____，测脉搏。

　　A 分钟　　　　B 秒　　　　　C °C

4 测呼吸要观察病人胸部的_____，30秒。

　　A 记录　　　　B 结果　　　　C 起伏

第 13 课 | 测量体温、脉搏和呼吸

学习语法 Grammar

语法点 1 Grammar Point 1

固定格式：（在）……前 / 后　Fixed structure: (在) ... 前 / 后

表示某事早于或晚于某个特定的时间，在句中做状语。
It means something happens before or after a specific time, used as an adverbial in a sentence.

例句：

1. Cèliáng tǐwēn, màibó hūxī qián, bìngrén yào xiūxi sānshí fēnzhōng.
测量体温、脉搏、呼吸前，病人要休息 30 分钟。
Before measuring body temperature, pulse, and respiration, patients should rest for 30 minutes.

2. Pínggū bìngrén de bìngqíng hòu, xiān bǎihǎo tǐwèi, zài jìnxíng qiǎngjiù.
评估病人的病情后，先摆好体位，再进行抢救。After assessing the patient's condition, first position him/her properly, then proceed with rescue.

3. Bìngrén xiūxi sānshí fēnzhōng hòu kěyǐ cèliáng tǐwēn.
病人休息 30 分钟后可以测量体温。After resting for 30 minutes, the patient's body temperature can be measured.

语法练习 1 Grammar Exercise 1

用 "……前 / 后" 完成句子。Complete the sentences with "... 前 / 后".

1. 测量体温、脉搏、呼吸　　病人要休息 30 分钟

_____

2. 摆好病人体位　　进行抢救

_____

3. 病人休息 30 分钟　　可以测呼吸

_____

121

4 登记轻症病人的基本信息　　安排就诊顺序

___

语法点 2 Grammar Point 2

特殊句型："把"字句 1　Special sentence pattern: the 把 -sentences 1

在谓语动词前使用介词短语"把+宾语"的句子叫作"把"字句。结构"把+宾语+动词+在/到+处所"表示主语通过动作行为使某个确定的事物位置发生移动。

A sentence that uses the prepositional phrase " 把 + object" before the predicate verb is called the 把 -sentence. The structure of " 把 + object + verb + 在 / 到 + location" indicates that the subject changes a certain object's position through the action.

例句：

1 把体温计的温度甩到 35℃ 以下。Swing the thermometer to make its temperature drop below 35℃.

2 把三个手指肚按在病人的桡动脉上。Press three finger pads on the patient's radial artery.

3 把检查结果记录在笔记本（notebook）上。Record the results of the assessment on a notebook.

语法练习 2 Grammar Exercise 2

按照正确的语序连词成句。Make sentences in correct orders with the given words or phrases.

1 ①把　②护士　③体温计的温度　④35℃以下　⑤甩到

第 13 课 | 测量体温、脉搏和呼吸

2 ①我 ②检查结果 ③把 ④记录在 ⑤笔记本上

_____

3 ①三个手指肚 ②把 ③按在 ④病人的桡动脉上

_____

4 ①马上 ②病人 ③把 ④重症监护室 ⑤送（sòng，send）到

_____

汉字书写 Writing Chinese Characters

jīn 巾 巾 巾
巾

bì 币 币 币 币
币

bù 布 布 布 布 布
布

diào 吊 吊 吊 吊 吊 吊
吊

123

文化拓展 Culture Insight

The Great Wall

The Great Wall is a monumental structure made of bricks and stones, standing tall and sturdy as it stretches across northern China. Like a giant dragon, it winds through steep mountains, plateaus, and deserts. The wall stretches over 20,000 kilometers and has a history of more than 2,200 years. Originally built as a military defense project to protect against invasions by northern nomadic tribes, the Great Wall was repaired and extended by various dynasties. The version we see today is primarily from the Ming Dynasty (1368–1644).

The Great Wall is a UNESCO World Heritage Site, celebrated for its rich history, impressive architecture, and embodiment of the resilient national spirit.

小结 Summary

词语 Words

朗读词语。Read the words aloud.

测量	体温计	手指肚
桡动脉	记录	结果

第 13 课 | 测量体温、脉搏和呼吸

语法 Grammar

朗读句子。Read the sentences aloud.

1. 在测量前病人要休息 30 分钟。
2. 护士把体温计的温度甩到 35℃ 以下。
3. 护士把手指肚按在病人桡动脉上。
4. 病人休息 30 分钟后可以测量呼吸。

课文理解 Text Comprehension

根据课文内容给下列句子排序。Put the statements in the correct order according to the text.

1. 测量脉搏，30 秒。
2. 病人休息 30 分钟。
3. 护士把体温计的温度甩到 35℃ 以下，测体温 5 分钟。
4. 测量呼吸，30 秒。
5. 记录体温、脉搏、呼吸的测量结果。

第14课 Lesson 14

Cèliáng xuèyā
测量血压
Measuring Blood Pressure

复习 Revision

朗读句子。Read the sentences aloud.

1. 测量体温、脉搏和呼吸前，病人要休息30分钟。
2. 把体温计的温度甩到35℃以下。
3. 把三个手指肚按在桡动脉上。
4. 观察病人胸部的起伏。

热身 Warming Up

看图选词。Look at the pictures and choose the correct words.

A 血压计 (xuèyājì) sphygmomanometer   B 手掌 (shǒuzhǎng) palm
C 手臂 (shǒubì) arm   D 心率 (xīnlǜ) heart rate

第 14 课 | 测量血压

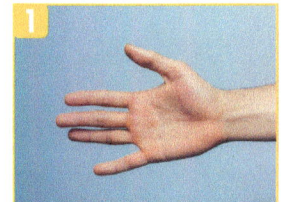

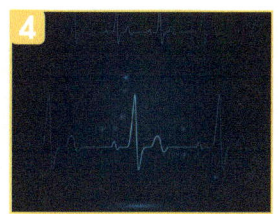

学习生词 Words and Expressions 🎧 14-1

1	伸	shēn	v.	extend
2	出	chū	v.	(used after a verb to indicate an outward direction)
3	右	yòu	n.	right
4	手臂	shǒubì	n.	arm
5	手掌	shǒuzhǎng	n.	palm
6	向	xiàng	prep.	towards
7	血压计	xuèyājì	n.	sphygmomanometer
8	袖带	xiùdài	n.	cuff
9	绑	bǎng	v.	tie
10	上臂	shàngbì	n.	upper arm
11	松紧	sōngjǐn	n.	tightness
12	容纳	róngnà	v.	accommodate

127

13	手指	shǒuzhǐ	n.	finger
14	启动	qǐdòng	v.	activate
15	结束	jiéshù	v.	end
16	显示	xiǎnshì	v.	display
17	显示屏	xiǎnshìpíng	n.	display screen
18	心率	xīnlǜ	n.	heart rate
19	关闭	guānbì	v.	turn off

词语练习 Words Exercises

1. 看图说词。Look at the pictures and say the words.

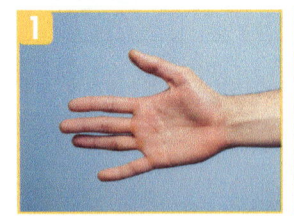

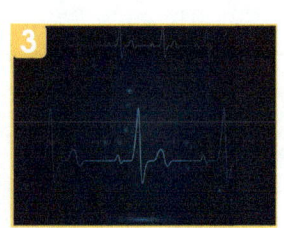

2. 朗读短语。Read the phrases aloud.

- 测量血压
- 伸出手臂
- 右手臂
- 右上臂
- 启动血压计
- 关闭血压计
- 显示血压
- 显示心率

学习课文 Text 🎧 14-2

测量血压
Cèliáng xuèyā

1. 病人伸出右手臂，手掌向上。
Bìngrén shēnchū yòu shǒubì, shǒuzhǎng xiàngshàng.

2. 把血压计袖带绑在病人右上臂，松紧为可以容纳一个手指。
Bǎ xuèyājì xiùdài bǎng zài bìngrén yòushàngbì, sōngjǐn wéi kěyǐ róngnà yí gè shǒuzhǐ.

3. 启动血压计。
Qǐdòng xuèyājì.

4. 测量结束，显示屏显示血压和心率。
Cèliáng jiéshù, xiǎnshìpíng xiǎnshì xuèyā hé xīnlǜ.

5. 关闭血压计。
Guānbì xuèyājì.

Measuring Blood Pressure

1. The patient extends his/her right arm with the palm facing upwards.

2. Tie the cuff of the sphygmomanometer on the patient's right upper arm, and the tightness can accommodate one finger.

3. Activate the sphygmomanometer.

4. The measurement ends, and the display screen shows the blood pressure and heart rate.

5. Turn off the sphygmomanometer.

课文练习 Text Exercises

1. 判断正误。True or false.

① 病人伸出左（zuǒ, left）手臂，手掌向上。
② 血压计袖带应该绑在病人的右上臂。
③ 血压计袖带松紧为可以容纳三个手指。
④ 测量结束，显示屏只显示血压。

2. 选词填空。Fill in the blanks with the correct words.

A 显示屏　　　B 血压计　　　C 向上　　　D 一个手指

① 测量血压，病人的右手掌_____。
② 护士把_____袖带绑在病人的右上臂。
③ 血压计绑带的松紧要能容纳下_____。
④ 测量结束后，_____显示血压和心率。

学习语法 Grammar

语法点 1 Grammar Point 1

补语：趋向补语 1　Complement: the complement of direction 1

"上、下、来、去、出、入、进"等单音节趋向动词，可以放在动词后面作补语，补充说明动作的趋向。

Monosyllabic verbs such as "上 (shàng, up), 下 (xià, down), 来 (lái, come), 去 (qù, go), 出 (chū, out), 入 (rù, into), 进 (jìn, in)" that indicate the tendency can be used as complements after a verb to supplement the direction of the action.

例句：
1. 病人伸出右手臂。The patient extended him/her right arm.
2. 护士拿（take）出血压计。The nurse takes out the sphygmomanometer.
3. 医生走进（zǒujìn, walk into）急诊大厅。The doctor walked into the emergency department lobby.

语法练习 1 Grammar Exercise 1

选词填空。Fill in the blanks with the correct words.

  A 上   B 下   C 出   D 进

1. 测量血压，病人伸_____右手臂。
2. 医生按_____血压计启动键（jiàn, key）测量血压。
3. 护士把袖带绑_____病人的右上臂。
4. 救护车把病人送_____医院。

语法点 2 Grammar Point 2

介词：向 Preposition: 向

介词"向"引介表示方向的词，表示动作的方向。

The preposition "向" introduces words that indicate direction, indicating the direction of the action.

例句：
1. 病人的 手掌 向上。 The patient's palm is facing upward.
   Bìngrén de shǒuzhǎng xiàngshàng.
2. 救护车 向 右 转（turn）。 The ambulance turns right.
   Jiùhùchē xiàng yòu zhuǎn.
3. 把三个手指肚向下 按在病人的桡动脉上。 Press three finger pads downwards on the patient's radial artery.
   Bǎ sān gè shǒuzhǐdù xiàngxià àn zài bìngrén de ráodòngmài shàng.

语法练习 2 Grammar Exercise 2

选择正确的词语，然后用"向"完成句子。Choose the correct words and complete the sentences with "向".

| A 上 | B 下 | C 前 | D 右 |

1. 测量血压，病人的手掌_____。
2. 三个手指肚_____按在病人的桡动脉上。
3. _____走是分诊台。
4. 从（cóng, from）观察室_____走是重症监护室。

汉字书写 Writing Chinese Characters

shī
尸 尸 尸
尸 尸 尸 尸 尸

第14课 | 测量血压

hù 户户户户
户 户 户 户 户

chǐ 尺尺尺尺
尺 尺 尺 尺 尺

hù 护护护护护护护
护 护 护 护 护

职业拓展 Career Insight

The Red Cross

The International Red Cross Movement has a history spanning over 150 years. It originated from battlefield rescue efforts and was founded by Henry Dunant, the father of the movement and the first recipient of the Nobel Peace Prize in 1901. The Red Cross is the international organization with the widest influence and the highest level of global recognition. It represents not just a spirit of humanitarian aid, but also a symbol that transcends borders, races, and beliefs, leading humanitarian efforts worldwide. The emblem of the International Red Cross features a red cross on a white background.

小结 Summary

词语 Words

朗读词语。Read the words aloud.

| 右臂—上臂 | 启动—关闭 |
| 心率 | 向上—向下 |

语法 Grammar

朗读句子。Read the sentences aloud.

1. 病人伸出右手臂。
2. 医生走进急诊大厅。
3. 手掌向上。
4. 把三个手指肚向下按在病人的桡动脉上。

课文理解 Text Comprehension

根据课文内容给下列句子排序。Put the statements in the correct order according to the text.

1. 护士把血压计袖带绑在病人右上臂。
2. 病人休息 30 分钟后测量血压。

第 14 课 | 测量血压

3 测量结束。

4 关闭血压计。

5 启动血压计。

_____

第15课 Lesson 15

测量血氧饱和度
Cèliáng xuèyǎng bǎohédù
Measuring Blood Oxygen Saturation

复习 Revision

朗读句子。Read the sentences aloud.

1. 病人伸出右手臂。
2. 病人手掌向上。
3. 把血压计袖带绑在病人右上臂。
4. 显示屏显示血压和心率。

热身 Warming Up

看图，学说五个手指的名称。Look at the picture and learn to say the names of five fingers.

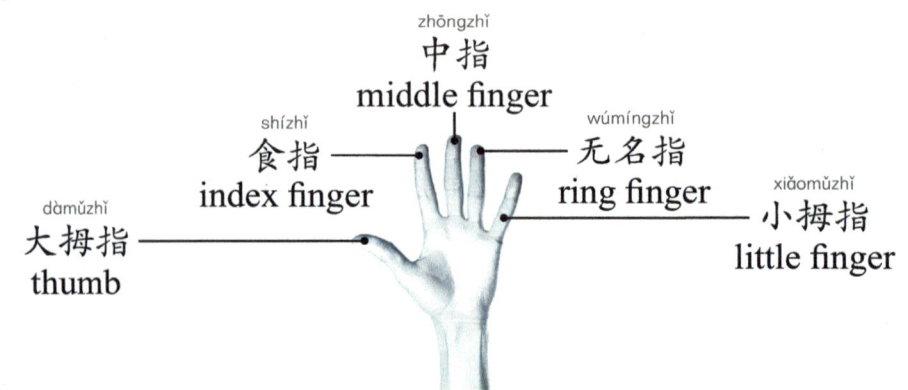

dàmǔzhǐ 大拇指 thumb

shízhǐ 食指 index finger

zhōngzhǐ 中指 middle finger

wúmíngzhǐ 无名指 ring finger

xiǎomǔzhǐ 小拇指 little finger

136

第 15 课 | 测量血氧饱和度

学习生词 Words and Expressions 🎧 15-1

1	检测仪	jiǎncèyí	n.	detector
2	就	jiù	adv.	exactly; precisely
3	血氧仪	xuèyǎngyí	n.	oximeter
4	如下	rúxià	v.	as follows
5	打开	dǎkāi	v.	open; turn on
6	开关	kāiguān	n.	switch
7	放入	fàngrù	v.	insert
8	食指	shízhǐ	n.	index finger
9	中指	zhōngzhǐ	n.	middle finger
10	或	huò	conj.	or
11	无名指	wúmíngzhǐ	n.	ring finger
12	指甲面	zhǐjiamiàn	n.	nail surface
13	进入	jìnrù	v.	enter
14	读取	dúqǔ	v.	read
15	正常值	zhèngchángzhí	n.	normal value
16	以上	yǐshàng	n.	above

137

词语练习 Words Exercises

1. 看图，说出五个手指的中文名称。Look at the picture and say the names of five fingers.

2. 朗读下列短语。Follow the words.

- 检测血氧饱和度
- 检测状态
- 读取数值
- 放入手指
- 取出手指
- 打开血氧仪
- 关闭血氧仪

学习课文 Text 15-2

Cèliáng xuèyáng bǎohédù
测量血氧饱和度

Xuèyáng bǎohédù　　　　　　　　jiǎncèyí　jiù shì xuèyǎngyí,
血氧饱和度（SpO2）检测仪就是血氧仪，
shǐyòng fāngfǎ rúxià:
使用方法如下：

Dǎkāi kāiguān.
1. 打开开关。

Fàngrù shǒuzhǐ:
2. 放入手指:

Bǎ bìngrén de shízhǐ, zhōngzhǐ huò wúmíngzhǐ fàngrù xuèyǎngyí.
把病人的食指、中指或无名指放入血氧仪。

Zhǐjiǎmiàn xiàngshàng.
指甲面向上。

Jiǎncè:
3. 检测:

Xuèyǎngyí jìnrù jiǎncè zhuàngtài. Sānshí miǎo hòu xiǎnshì cèliáng jiéguǒ.
血氧仪进入检测状态。30秒后显示测量结果。

Dúqǔ shùzhí:
4. 读取数值:

Xiǎnshìpíng shàng de shùzhí shì xuèyǎng hé xīnlǜ. Xuèyǎng de
显示屏上的数值是血氧和心率。血氧的

zhèngchángzhí zài bǎi fēnzhī jiǔshíwǔ yǐshàng.
正常值在 95% 以上。

Qǔchū shǒuzhǐ, guānbì kāiguān.
5. 取出手指,关闭开关。

Measuring Blood Oxygen Saturation

The SpO2 detector is an oximeter, and the way to use it is as follows:

1. Turn on the switch.

2. Insert the finger:

Put the patient's index finger, middle finger, or ring finger into the oximeter, with the nail facing upwards.

3. Detect:

The oximeter enters the detection state, and displays the result of the measurement after 30 seconds.

4. Read the numerical values:

The values on the display screen are blood oxygen and heart rate. The normal value of blood oxygen is above 95%.

5. Take out the finger and turn off the switch.

课文练习 Text Exercises

1. 判断正误。True or false.

1 血氧仪是血氧饱和度（SpO2）检测仪。

2 测量血氧饱和度时，指甲面向上。

3 显示屏上的数值是血氧和心率。

4 血氧的正常值在 95% 以下。

2. 选词填空。Fill in the blanks with the correct answers.

1 把病人的_____、中指或无名指放入血氧仪。

　　A 食指　　　　B 指甲　　　　C 上臂

2 指甲面向_____。

　　A 下　　　　　B 上　　　　　C 前

3 显示屏上的_____是血氧和心率。

　　A 测量　　　　B 数值　　　　C 开关

4 血氧的_____在 95% 以上。

　　A 状态　　　　B 数值　　　　C 正常值

第 15 课 | 测量血氧饱和度

学习语法 Grammar

语法点 1 Grammar Point 1

连词：或　Conjunction: 或

"或"连接词或短语，表示从二者或多者中选择其一。

The conjunction "或" is used to connect words or phrases to indicate choosing one of two or more.

例句：

1. Bǎ bìngrén de shízhǐ, zhōngzhǐ huò wúmíngzhǐ fàngrù xuèyǎngyí.
   把病人的食指、中指或无名指放入血氧仪。Put the patient's index finger, middle finger, or ring finger into the oximeter.

2. Cèliáng tǐwēn, màibó huò hūxī qián, bìngrén yào xiūxi sānshí fēnzhōng.
   测量体温、脉搏或呼吸前，病人要休息 30 分钟。Before measuring the body temperature, pulse, or respiration, patients should rest for 30 minutes.

3. Sānshíliù shèshìdù huò sānshíqī shèshìdù dōu shì zhèngcháng tǐwēn.
   36°C 或 37°C 都是正常体温。Both 36°C and 37°C are normal body temperatures.

语法练习 1 Grammar Exercise 1

把"或"放在句中合适的位置。Put "或" in the right place in the sentence.

1. 把病人的____食指、____中指____无名指____放入血氧仪。

2. 测量____体温、____脉搏____呼吸前，病人____要休息30分钟。

3. 您____对什么____药物____食物____过敏？

4. ____脉搏____每分钟80____90次____正常吗？

141

语法点 2 Grammar Point 2

特殊句型：" 把 " 字句 2 Special sentence pattern: the 把 -sentences 2

结构 " 把 + 宾语 + 动词 + 趋向补语 +（处所）" 表示主语通过动作行为使某个事物的位置朝某个方向移动。

The structure of " 把 + object + verb + directional complement + (location)" indicates that the subject moves the position of something in a certain direction through action.

例句：

1. 把病人的手指放入血氧仪。Put the patient's finger into the oximeter.
   Bǎ bìngrén de shǒuzhǐ fàngrù xuèyǎngyí.

2. 把病人的手指取出，关闭开关。Take out the patient's finger and turn off the switch.
   Bǎ bìngrén de shǒuzhǐ qǔchū, guānbì kāiguān.

3. 把病人抬（lift）进救护车。Lift the patient into the ambulance.
   Bǎ bìngrén tái jìn jiùhùchē.

语法练习 2 Grammar Exercise 2

按照正确的语序连词成句。Make sentences in correct orders with the given words or phrases.

1. ①取出 ②把 ③病人的手指 ④医生

   _____

2. ①把 ②血氧仪 ③放入 ④病人的手指 ⑤护士

   _____

3. ①把 ②病人 ③放进 ④温度计 ⑤腋下（yèxià, armpit）

   _____

4 ①急诊室　②病人　③推（tuī，push）进　④把

_____

汉字书写 Writing Chinese Characters

nǚ 女女女
女

zǐ 子子子
子

hǎo 好好好好好好
好

ān 安安安安安安
安

文化拓展 Culture Insight

The Forbidden City

The Forbidden City, located in the heart of Beijing, China's capital, served as the imperial palace for 24 emperors during the Ming (1368–1644) and Qing (1644–1911) dynasties. With a history spanning over 600 years, it covers an area of approximately 720,000 square meters. It is the largest and most well-preserved ancient architectural and palace complex in China, renowned for its exquisite design and as a masterpiece of ancient architecture.

The Forbidden City is also home to a vast collection of cultural relics and artworks, including paintings, ceramics, jade artifacts, and other treasures. Among its most famous features is the Palace Museum, one of the largest museums of ancient art in the world. The Forbidden City is a UNESCO World Heritage Site, celebrated globally for its historical and cultural significance.

小结 Summary

词语 Words

朗读词语。Read the words aloud.

血氧饱和度	血氧仪	状态
读取	正常值	手指

语法 Grammar

朗读句子。Read the sentences aloud.

1. 放入手指或无名指。
2. 病人的中指或无名指的指甲面向上。
3. 把病人的食指或无名指放入血氧仪。
4. 把病人抬进救护车。

课文理解 Text Comprehension

根据课文内容给下列句子排序。Put the statements in the correct order according to the text.

1. 放入手指，指甲面向上。
2. 打开开关。
3. 检测，30秒。
4. 取出手指，关闭开关。
5. 读取血氧和心率数值。

第16课 Lesson 16

紧急救护 Jǐnjí jiùhù
Emergency Care

复习 Revision

选词填空。Fill in the blanks with the correct words.

1. 血氧饱和度_____仪就是血氧仪。

    A 检测　　　　B 打开　　　　C 扭伤

2. 把病人的_____放入血氧仪。

    A 体位　　　　B 食指　　　　C 皮肤

3. 显示屏上的_____是血氧和心率。

    A 数值　　　　B 心跳　　　　C 食指

4. 血氧的正常值在_____以上。

    A 30%　　　　B 70%　　　　C 95%

第 16 课 | 紧急救护

热身 Warming Up

看图选词。Look at the pictures and choose the correct words.

A 气管 (qìguǎn) trachea　　B 气管插管 (qìguǎn chāguǎn) tracheal cannula
C 输血 (shūxiě) blood transfusion　　D 呼吸机 (hūxījī) respirator

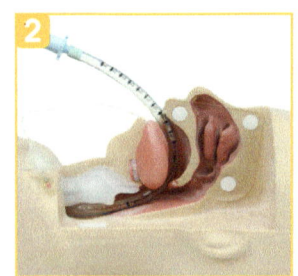

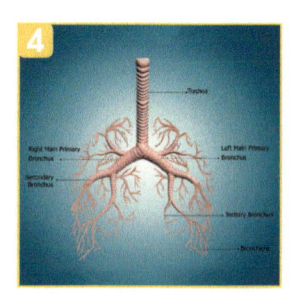

1　2　3　4

学习生词 Words and Expressions 🎧 16-1

1	紧急	jǐnjí	adj.	emergent
2	通气	tōngqì	v.	ventilate
3	清除	qīngchú	v.	remove
4	异物	yìwù	n.	foreign body
5	自主	zìzhǔ	v.	spontaneous

6	开放	kāifàng	v.	open
7	插入	chārù	v.	insert
8	管	guǎn	n.	tube
9	必要	bìyào	adj.	necessary
10	时	shí	n.	time
11	气管插管	qìguǎn chāguǎn		tracheal cannula
12	连接	liánjiē	v.	connect
13	呼吸机	hūxījī	n.	respirator
14	止血	zhǐxiě	v.	hemostasis
15	输液	shūyè	v.	infusion
16	两	liǎng	num.	two
17	输血	shūxiě	v.	blood transfusion

词语练习 Words Exercises

1. 看图说词。 Look at the pictures and say the words.

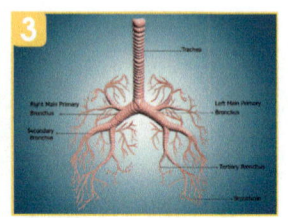

第 16 课 | 紧急救护

2. 朗读短语。Read the phrases aloud.

| 紧急救护 | 自主呼吸 | 清除异物 |
| 开放气道 | 插入通气管 | 连接呼吸机 |

学习课文 Text 🎧 16-2

Jǐnjí jiùhù
紧急救护

Jǐnjí qiǎngjiù suíshí yǒu shēngmìng wēixiǎn de bìngrén, cuòshī
紧急抢救随时有生命危险的病人，措施
rúxià:
如下：

1. Tōngqì:
通气：
Qīngchú qìdào yìwù. Méiyǒu zìzhǔ hūxī de bìngrén, kāifàng
清除气道异物。没有自主呼吸的病人，开放
qìdào, mǎshàng chārù tōngqìguǎn, bìyào shí shǐyòng qìguǎn
气道，马上插入通气管，必要时使用气管
chāguǎn, liánjiē hūxījī.
插管，连接呼吸机。

2. Xīyǎng.
吸氧。

3. Zhǐxiě.
止血。

4. Shūyè:
输液：

149

建立两个静脉通道，输液、输血。

5. 监测：

监测呼吸、循环和意识。

Emergency Care

Emergency rescue measures for patients who are at risk of life at any time are as follows:

1. Ventilation:

Remove foreign bodies from the airway. For patients without spontaneous breathing, open the airway and immediately insert a ventilation tube. If necessary, use a tracheal cannula and connect to the ventilator.

2. Oxygen inhalation.

3. Hemostasis.

4. Infusion:

Establish two venous accesses for infusion and blood transfusion.

5. Monitoring:

Monitor breathing, circulation, and consciousness.

第 16 课 | 紧急救护

课文练习 Text Exercises

1. 判断正误。True or false.

① 随时有生命危险的病人，要进行紧急救护。

② 开放气道后，马上插入通气管。

③ 给病人建立一个静脉通道。

④ 监测病人的呼吸、循环和意识。

2. 选词填空。Fill in the blanks with the correct words.

① 没有自主呼吸的病人，开放_____。
   A 气道　　　　B 插管　　　　C 通气管

② 建立两个静脉通道，_____、输血。
   A 吸氧　　　　B 止血　　　　C 输液

③ 清除气道后，必要时使用_____插管，连接呼吸机。
   A 气管　　　　B 呼吸　　　　C 脉搏

④ 监测呼吸、循环和_____。
   A 气管　　　　B 脉搏　　　　C 意识

学习语法 Grammar

语法点 1 Grammar Point 1

名词：时　Noun: 时

"……时"表示在某个特定的时点或时段。一般在句中作状语。

"... 时" means at a specific point or time period. It is usually used as an adverbial in a sentence.

151

例句：
① 必要时使用气管插管。Use a tracheal cannula if necessary.
　　　Bìyào shí shǐyòng qìguǎn chāguǎn.

② 紧急抢救病人时，要先通气。When rescuing a patient in an emergency, ventilation is necessary first.
　　Jǐnjí qiǎngjiù bìngrén shí, yào xiān tōngqì.

③ 输液时，要建立两个静脉通道。When infusing, two venous accesses should be established.
　　Shūyè shí, yào jiànlì liǎng gè jìngmài tōngdào.

语法练习 1 Grammar Exercise 1

用"……时"完成句子。Complete the sentences with "… 时".

① 必要　　使用气管插管

_____

② 紧急抢救病人　　要先通气

_____

③ 输液　　要建立两个静脉通道

_____

④ 病人休克　　要马上抢救

_____

语法点 2 Grammar Point 2

数词：二 / 两　Numerals: 二 / 两

个位数在一般量词前用"两"。
For single-digit numbers, "两" is used before common measure words.

例句：① 建立两个静脉通道。Establish two venous accesses.
　　　　Jiànlì liǎng gè jìngmài tōngdào.

> Tāmen liǎng gè rén dōu shì yīshēng.
> 2. 他们两个人都是医生。Both of them are doctors.
>
> Zhè ge bìngrén yǐqián zuòguò liǎng cì shǒushù.
> 3. 这个病人以前做过两次手术。This patient has had two surgeries before.

语法练习 2 Grammar Exercise 2

选词填空。Fill in the blanks with the correct words.

A 二　　　　　　B 两

1. 救护车 12（读"十_____"）点赶到病人家里。
2. 这_____个数值是血氧和心率。
3. 2（读"_____"）是什么疼痛程度？
4. 病人以前做过_____次手术。

汉字书写 Writing Chinese Characters

yě
也 也 也 也

tā
他 他 他 他 他 他

dì	地 地 地 地 地 地
地	地 地 地 地

tā	她 她 她 她 她 她
她	她 她 她 她

职业拓展 Career Insight

Angel in White

In China, "Angel in white" is a nickname for nurses. Most nurses wear white work clothes, which are fresh, clean, safe, hygienic, and have a calming effect; White gives people a feeling of holiness, tranquility, peace, and holiness. In Western mythology, angels are holy and helpful. Engaging in the sacred cause of saving lives and aiding the wounded brings hope and happiness to humanity, hence the nickname "Angel in white" for nurses.

小结 Summary

词语 Words

朗读词语。Read the words aloud.

| 输液—输血 | 通气 | 异物 | 开放 |
| 气管插管 | 呼吸机 | 静脉通道 | 自主呼吸 |

语法 Grammar

朗读句子。Read the sentences aloud.

1. 必要时使用气管插管。
2. 必要时连接呼吸机。
3. 建立两个静脉通道。
4. 他做过两次手术。

课文理解 Text Comprehension

根据课文内容给下列句子排序。Put the statements in the correct order according to the text.

1. 止血。
2. 吸氧。
3. 通气，清除气道异物、插管、连接呼吸机等。
4. 监测呼吸、循环和意识。
5. 输液、输血。

Unit 3 外伤救护技术

Wàishāng jiùhù jìshù

Trauma Rescue Techniques

第三单元

第17课 Lesson 17

外伤止血 (Wàishāng zhǐxiě)
Trauma Hemostasis

复习 Revision

朗读句子。Read the sentences aloud.

1. 抢救随时有生命危险的病人。
2. 清除气道异物。必要时使用气管插管。
3. 建立两个静脉通道，输液、输血。
4. 监测呼吸、循环和意识。

热身 Warming Up

看图选词。Look at the pictures and choose the correct words.

A 包扎 (bāozā) bandage 　　B 面 (miàn) face
C 止血带 (zhǐxiědài) tourniquet　D 尺动脉 (chǐdòngmài) ulnar artery

第 17 课 | 外伤止血

学习生词 Words and Expressions 🎧 17-1

1	应该	yīnggāi	v.	should
2	出血量	chūxiěliàng	n.	amount of hemorrhaging
3	太	tài	adv.	too
4	多	duō	adj.	much; many
5	指压法	zhǐyāfǎ	n.	finger-pressing manipulation
6	加压	jiāyā	v.	apply pressure
7	包扎	bāozā	v.	bandage
8	止血带	zhǐxiědài	n.	tourniquet
9	手	shǒu	n.	hand
10	按压	ànyā	v.	press

11	达到	dádào	v.	achieve
12	目的	mùdì	n.	goal
13	面	miàn	n.	face
14	压迫	yāpò	v.	compress
15	尺动脉	chǐdòngmài	n.	ulnar artery
16	效果	xiàoguǒ	n.	effect

词语练习 Words Exercises

1. 看图说词。 Look at the pictures and say the words.

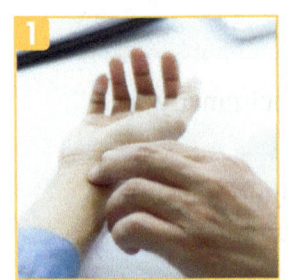

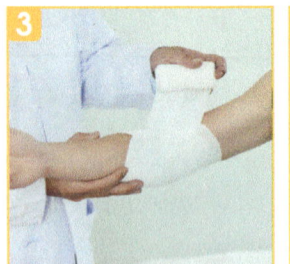

2. 朗读词语搭配。 Read the collocations aloud.

- 手部出血
- 面部出血
- 外伤出血
- 快速止血
- 面动脉
- 出血量太多

学习课文 Text 🎧 17-2

外伤止血
Wàishāng zhǐxiě

外伤出血应该快速处理。出血量太多,病人会休克。止血方法有指压法、加压包扎法和止血带止血法。指压法是用手指按压血管,达到止血的目的。例如,手部出血时可以压迫尺动脉和桡动脉;面部出血时可以压迫面动脉。指压法是紧急措施,效果不太好。

Traumatic Hemostasis

Traumatic hemorrhaging should be treated quickly. Excessive bleeding can cause a shock for the patient. The methods of hemostasis include finger-pressing manipulation, pressure bandaging, and hemostasis with tourniquet. Finger-pressing manipulation is to use fingers to press blood vessels to achieve the goal of hemostasis. For example, for hand bleeding, compress the ulnar and radial arteries; facial bleeding, compress the facial artery. Finger-pressing manipulation is an emergency measure, which doesn't work very well.

课文练习 Text Exercises

1. 判断正误。True or false.

① 外伤出血应该快速止血。

② 加压包扎法是一种止血法。

③ 手部出血可以压迫尺动脉。

④ 指压法效果很（hěn，very）好。

2. 选词填空。Fill in the blanks with the correct words.

| A 动脉 | B 紧急 | C 止血带 | D 出血量 |

① _____太多，病人会休克。

② 止血方法有指压法、加压包扎法、_____止血法。

③ 面部出血可以压迫面_____。

④ 指压法是_____措施。

第 17 课 | 外伤止血

学习语法 Grammar

语法点 1 Grammar Point 1

能愿动词：应该　Modal verb: 应该

"应该"后接动词，表示情理上是理所应当的。
"应该" is followed by a verb, indicating that something is necessarily so in a logical and emotional way.

例句：
1. Wàishāng chūxiě yīnggāi kuàisù chǔlǐ.
外伤出血应该快速处理。Traumatic hemorrhaging should be treated quickly.

2. Jiùhù suíshí yǒu shēngmìng wēixiǎn de bìngrén, yīnggāi mǎshàng qīngchú qìdào yìwù.
救护随时有生命危险的病人，应该马上清除气道异物。To rescue the patient who is at risk of life at any time, the foreign bodies of the airway must be removed immediately.

3. Bìngrén de zhǐjiǎmiàn yīnggāi xiàngshàng.
病人的指甲面应该向上。The patient's nail surface should be facing upwards.

语法练习 1 Grammar Exercise 1

选择正确的答案。Choose the correct answers.

A 快速处理　　B 向上　　C 清除气道异物　　D 容纳一个手指

1. 外伤出血应该_____。
2. 量血压时病人的指甲面应该_____。

163

3 救护随时有生命危险的病人，应该_____。

4 绑血压计时，松紧应该能_____。

语法点 2　Grammar Point 2

副词：太　　Adverb: 太

副词"太"可以表示程度过分，放在形容词前面。结构"太……了"表示感叹程度高。
The adverb "太" indicates an excessive degree, used before an adjective. The structure "太 ... 了" indicates a high degree of exclamation.

例句：
1 _{Chūxiěliàng tài duō, bìngrén huì xiūkè.}
出血量太多，病人会休克。Excessive bleeding can cause a shock for the patient.

2 _{Tài hǎo le! Bìngrén ānquán　　　 le.}
太好了！病人安全（safe）了。Great! The patient is safe.

3 _{Zhǐyāfǎ shì jǐnjí cuòshī, xiàoguǒ bú tài hǎo.}
指压法是紧急措施，效果不太好。Finger-pressing manipulation is an emergency measure, which doesn't work very well.

语法练习 2　Grammar Exercise 2

把"太"放在句中合适的位置。Put "太" in the right place in the sentence.

1 ____出血量____多，病人____会____休克。

2 指压法____是紧急措施，____效果不____好____。

3 ____血压____高，需要____马上____抢救。

4 病人____的病情____严重____了____。

汉字书写 Writing Chinese Characters

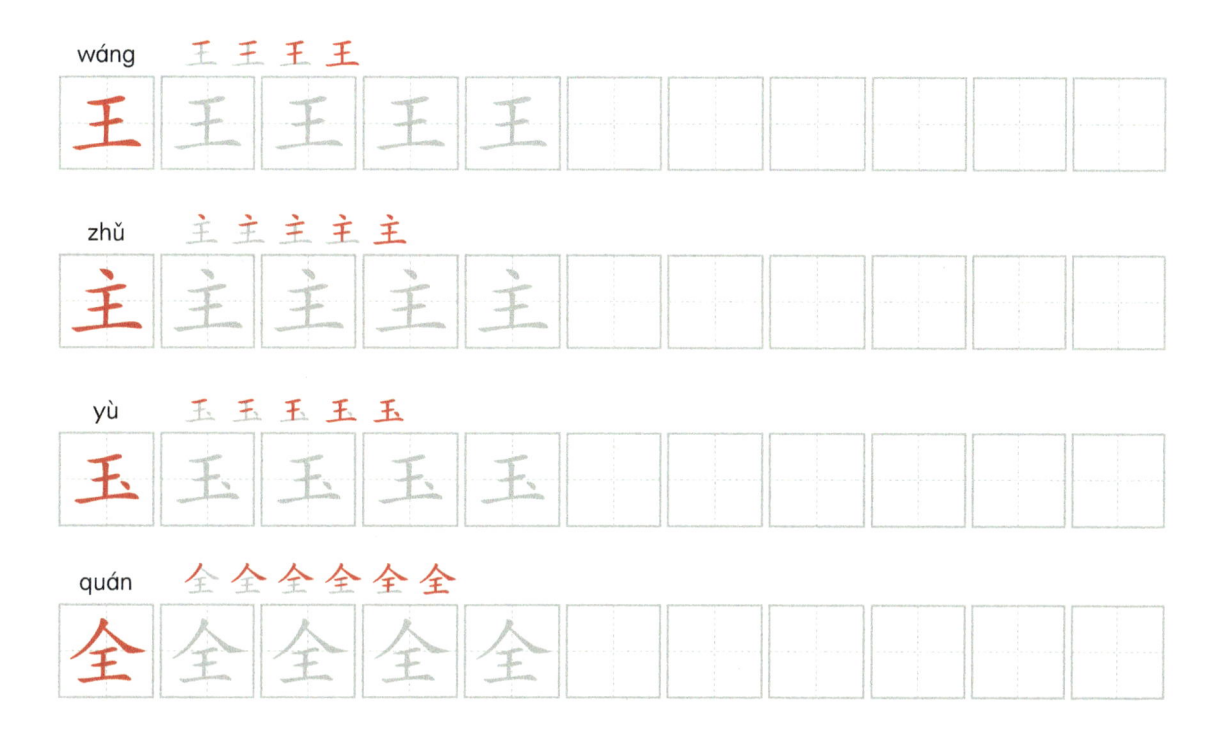

wáng
王 王 王 王
王 王 王 王 王

zhǔ
主 主 主 主 主
主 主 主 主 主

yù
玉 玉 玉 玉 玉
玉 玉 玉 玉 玉

quán
全 全 全 全 全 全
全 全 全 全 全

文化拓展 Culture Insight

One of the Four Great Inventions of Ancient China: Compass

Papermaking, the compass, gunpowder, and movable type printing are universally recognized as the Four Great Inventions of ancient China. These represent the intellectual achievements and technological innovations of ancient China, greatly advancing its political, economic, and cultural development. Through various channels, these inventions spread to the West, exerting a profound influence on world history and civilization.

The compass, an instrument used to determine orientation, evolved from an earlier device called Sinan. The magnetic needle on a compass points toward the geographic North Pole under the influence of the Earth's magnetic field. The compass likely emerged during the Warring States period (476–221 BC) and was used in military strategy, rituals, divination, and fengshui. By the Xuanhe period of the Northern Song Dynasty (1119–1125), it was being used for maritime navigation, significantly enhancing the safety and reach of sea travel.

小结 Summary

词语 Words

朗读词语。Read the words aloud.

出血量	指压法	包扎
止血带	尺动脉	面动脉

语法 Grammar

朗读句子。Read the sentences aloud.

1. 出血量太多，病人会休克。
2. 效果不太好。
3. 外伤出血应该快速处理。

4 手部出血应该压迫尺动脉和桡动脉。

课文理解 Text Comprehension

根据课文内容选词填空。Fill in the blanks with correct words according to the text.

> A 按压   B 快速   C 效果   D 尺动脉   E 止血带

外伤出血应该_____处理。止血方法有指压法、加压包扎法和_____止血法。指压法是用手指_____血管，达到止血的目的。手部出血可以压迫_____和桡动脉。指压法是紧急措施，_____不太好。

第18课 Lesson 18

止血带止血 (Zhǐxiědài zhǐxiě)
Hemostasis with Tourniquet

复习 Revision

朗读句子。Read the sentences aloud.

1. 外伤出血应该快速处理。
2. 出血量太多，病人会休克。
3. 止血方法有指压法、加压包扎法和止血带止血法。
4. 指压法是用手指按压血管。

热身 Warming Up

看图选词。Look at the pictures and choose the correct words.

A 缠绕 (chánrào) wrap	B 时间 (shíjiān) time
C 上肢 (shàngzhī) upper limb	D 打活结 (dǎ huójié) tie a slip knot

第18课 | 止血带止血

学习生词 Words and Expressions 🎧 18-1

1	只	zhǐ	*adv.*	only
2	适用于	shìyòngyú		be applicable to
3	以……为	yǐ…wéi		take…as…
4	例	lì	*n.*	example
5	上肢	shàngzhī	*n.*	upper limb
6	棉垫	miándiàn	*n.*	cotton pad
7	缠绕	chánrào	*v.*	wrap
8	处	chù	*n.*	place
9	打活结	dǎ huójié		tie a slip knot
10	搏动	bódòng	*v.*	pulse
11	成功	chénggōng	*v.*	succeed
12	贴	tiē	*v.*	stick
13	标签	biāoqiān	*n.*	label
14	写	xiě	*v.*	write
15	时间	shíjiān	*n.*	time

169

16	通常	tōngcháng	adv.	usually
17	放松	fàngsōng	v.	loosen
18	超过	chāoguò	v.	exceed
19	小时	xiǎoshí	n.	hour

词语练习 Words Exercises

1. 看图说词。 Look at the pictures and say the words.

2. 朗读短语。 Read the phrases aloud.

- 止血成功
- 缠绕止血带
- 放松止血带
- 打一个活结
- 贴上标签
- 四肢的大动脉

学习课文 Text 18-2

Zhǐxiědài zhǐxiě
止血带止血

Zhǐxiědài zhǐxiěfǎ zhǐ shìyòngyú sìzhī dàdòngmài。 Yǐ shàngzhī
止血带止血法只适用于四肢大动脉。以上肢

为例：

1. 把棉垫缠绕在病人上臂上 1/3 处。

2. 在棉垫上缠绕止血带，打活结。桡动脉没有搏动，止血成功。

3. 贴上标签，写上操作时间。

4. 通常每 30 分钟放松止血带 2 分钟。连续止血时间不要超过 5 小时。

Hemostasis with Tourniquet

The hemostasis with tourniquet is only applicable to the large arteries of the limbs. Take the upper limbs as an example:

1. Wrap the cotton pad around 1/3 of the patient's upper arm.

2. Wrap a tourniquet around the cotton pad and tie a slip knot. The radial artery does not pulse and the hemostasis succeeds.

3. Stick a label and write down the operating time.

4. Usually, loosen the tourniquet for 2 minutes every 30 minutes. The time of hemostasis can't sustain more than 5 hours.

课文练习 Text Exercises

1. 判断正误。True or false.

① 止血带止血法适用于全身。

② 把棉垫缠绕在病人上臂上 1/3 处。

③ 缠绕止血带时打活结。

④ 通常每 15 分钟放松止血带 2 分钟。

2. 根据课文内容回答问题。Answer the questions according to the text.

① 止血带止血法适用于什么部位的止血？

_____

② 上肢出血时止血带的棉垫缠绕在什么部位？

_____

③ 什么情况是止血成功？

_____

④ 连续止血不要超过多长时间？

_____

学习语法 Grammar

语法点 1 Grammar Point 1

副词：只 Adverb: 只

副词"只"表示仅仅、唯一，或仅限于某个范围。
The adverb "只" means "only, just", or the limitation to a certain scope.

例句：
1. Zhǐxiědài zhǐxiěfǎ zhǐ shìyòngyú sìzhī dàdòngmài.
   止血带止血法只适用于四肢大动脉。The hemostasis with tourniquet is only applicable to the large arteries of the limbs.
2. Nǐ bù néng zhǐ chī cài.
   你不能只吃菜（vegetable）。You shouldn't only eat vegetables.
3. Zhǐyāfǎ zhǐ shì jǐnjí cuòshī, xiàoguǒ bú tài hǎo.
   指压法只是紧急措施，效果不太好。The finger-pressing manipulation is only an emergency measure, which doesn't work very well.

语法练习 1 Grammar Exercise 1

把"只"放在句中合适的位置。Put "只" in the right place in the sentence.

1. 这种____止血法____适用于____四肢大动脉____止血。
2. ____指压法____是____紧急措施，效果不____太好。
3. 病人____有____呼吸和心跳，____没有____意识。
4. ____重症监护室____护理病情____最严重____的病人。

语法点 2 Grammar Point 2

固定格式：以……为…… Fixed structure: 以 ... 为 ...

"以……为……"意思是"把……作为……"。
"以 ... 为 ..." means "regard...as...".

例句：
1. Yǐ shàngzhī wéi lì, zhǐxiědài zhǐxiěfǎ yǒu sì gè bùzhòu.
   以上肢为例，止血带止血法有四个步骤（step）。
   Taking the upper limb as an example, the hemostasis with tourniquet has four steps.

② 以头部为例，次级评估需要检查外伤、眼、耳、鼻和神经系统。Taking the head as an example, the secondary assessment requires examination of trauma, eyes, ears, nose, and nervous system.

③ 生命体征包括体温、脉搏等。以体温为例，体温正常范围为36—37℃。Vital signs include body temperature, pulse, etc. Taking body temperature as an example, the normal range of body temperature is 36–37°C.

语法练习 2 Grammar Exercise 2

用"以……为例"完成句子。Complete the sentences with "以 ... 为例".

① 上肢　　止血带止血法有四个步骤

_____

② 手部　　止血可以压迫尺动脉和桡动脉止血

_____

③ 面部出血　　压迫面动脉可以止血

_____

④ 头部检查　　需要检查外伤、眼、耳、鼻和神经系统

_____

第18课 | 止血带止血

汉字书写 Writing Chinese Characters

kāi 开 开 开 开
开

tiān 天 天 天 天
天

guān 关 关 关 关 关 关
关

bìng 并 并 并 并 并 并
并

职业拓展 Career Insight

International Nurses Day

Florence Nightingale (May 12, 1820 – August 13, 1910) is recognized as the founder of modern nursing and nursing education. She opened a battlefield hospital to care for wounded soldiers, becoming the world's first true professional female nurse. Nightingale also founded the first formal nursing school and introduced a scientific theory of nursing. Her name, "Nightingale," has come to symbolize the spirit of nurses' dedication to

175

saving lives and helping the injured. The oath she wrote for nurses is known as the Nightingale Oath.

  International Nurses Day is celebrated on her birthday, May 12th. The International Red Cross established the Nightingale Medal, which is the highest honor awarded globally for outstanding contributions to nursing.

小结 Summary

词语 Words

朗读词语。Read the words aloud.

上肢	缠绕	搏动
放松	打活结	贴标签

语法 Grammar

朗读句子。Read the sentences aloud.

1. 止血带止血法只适用于四肢大动脉出血。
2. 指压法只是紧急措施。
3. 以上肢为例，止血带止血法的方法是……
4. 以头部为例，次级评估需要检查外伤、眼、耳、鼻和神经系统。

第18课 | 止血带止血

课文理解 Text Comprehension

根据课文内容给下列句子排序。Put the statements in the correct order according to the text.

1. 在棉垫上缠绕止血带，打活结。
2. 贴上标签，写上操作时间。
3. 在病人上臂缠绕棉垫。
4. 每30分钟放松止血带2分钟。
5. 观察桡动脉，没有搏动，止血成功。

第19课 Lesson 19

Wàishāng bāozā
外伤包扎
Trauma Dressing

复习 Revision

选词填空。Fill in the blanks with the correct words.

1. 止血带止血法_____适用于四肢大动脉出血。

   A 都　　　　　B 只　　　　　C 所有

2. 把棉垫_____在病人上臂上1/3处。

   A 适用　　　　B 成功　　　　C 缠绕

3. 桡动脉没有_____，止血成功。

   A 操作　　　　B 搏动　　　　C 超过

4. _____止血不要超过5小时。

   A 放松　　　　B 标签　　　　C 连续

第 19 课 | 外伤包扎

热身 Warming Up

将图片和对应词语连线。Match the pictures with corresponding words.

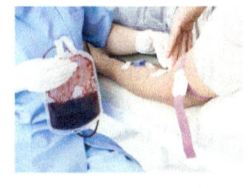

1 •   • 血液 blood (xuèyè)

2 •   • 绷带 bandage (bēngdài)

3 •   • 苍白 pale (cāngbái)

4 •   • 固定 fixed (gùdìng)

5 •   • 青紫 black and blue (qīngzǐ)

6 •   • 肿胀 swell (zhǒngzhàng)

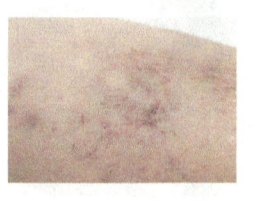

179

学习生词 Words and Expressions 🎧 19-1

1	绷带	bēngdài	n.	bandage
2	三角巾	sānjiǎojīn	n.	triangular bandage
3	悬吊	xuándiào	v.	suspend
4	既……也……	jì...yě...		both...and...
5	固定	gùdìng	adj.	fixed
6	更	gèng	adv.	more
7	这样	zhèyàng	pron.	like this
8	减轻	jiǎnqīng	v.	alleviate
9	肿胀	zhǒngzhàng	v.	swell
10	适宜	shìyí	adj.	appropriate
11	会	huì	v.	can
12	影响	yǐngxiǎng	v.	affect
13	血液	xuèyè	n.	blood
14	苍白	cāngbái	adj.	pale
15	青紫	qīngzǐ	adj.	black and blue
16	说明	shuōmíng	v.	indicate

词语练习 Words Exercises

1. 看图说词。 Look at the pictures and say the words.

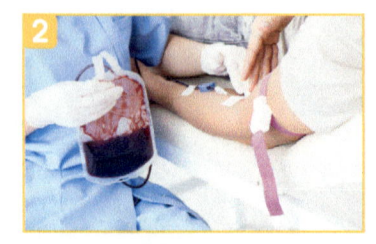

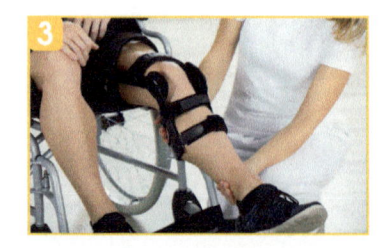

第 19 课 | 外伤包扎

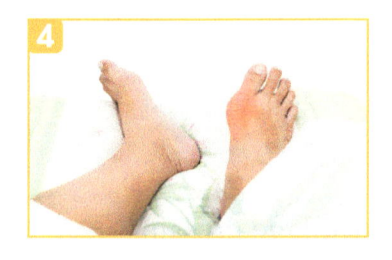

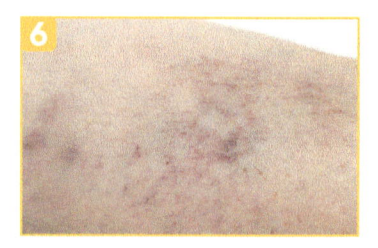

2. 朗读短语。Read the phrases aloud.

绷带包扎 三角巾包扎 悬吊包扎

使用绷带包扎 使用三角巾包扎 减轻肿胀

松紧适宜 影响血液循环

学习课文 Text 19-2

Wàishāng bāozā
外伤 包扎

外伤包扎的方法有绷带包扎、三角巾包扎和悬吊包扎。悬吊包扎既使用绷带，也使用三角巾，三角巾的固定效果更好。包扎时应该抬高患肢，这样可以减轻肿胀。包扎时要松紧适宜，这样不会影响血液循环。病人手指苍白或青紫，说明包扎太紧，应该放松。

181

Trauma Dressing

The methods of trauma dressing include bandage dressing, triangular bandage dressing, and suspension dressing. Suspension dressing uses both bandages and triangular bandages which have a better fixing effect. When dressing, the affected limb should be raised to alleviate swelling. When dressing, the tightness should be appropriate, so as not to affect blood circulation. The patient's fingers are pale or blue, indicating that the dressing is too tight and should be loosened.

课文练习 Text Exercises

1. 判断正误。True or false.

1. 外伤包扎的方法有三个。
2. 悬吊包扎只使用绷带。
3. 包扎时应该抬高患肢。
4. 病人手指苍白,说明应该放松。

2. 根据课文内容回答问题。Answer the questions according to the text.

1. 外伤包扎的方法有什么?

2. 悬吊包扎用什么固定效果更好?

3. 包扎时为什么（wèi shénme, why）抬高患肢？

_____

4. 包扎后，病人手指青紫，说明什么？

_____

学习语法 Grammar

语法点 1 Grammar Point 1

> 并列复句：既……也……　Coordinate complex sentence: 既 ... 也 ...
>
> "既……也……"连接并列的两个分句，表示主语同时具备两个方面。
> "既 ... 也 ..." connects two coordinate clauses, indicating the subject has two aspects.
>
> 例句：
> 1. 悬吊包扎既使用绷带，也使用三角巾。Suspension dressing uses both bandages and triangular bandages.
>   *Xuándiào bāozā jì shǐyòng bēngdài, yě shǐyòng sānjiǎojīn.*
> 2. 包扎时既不要太紧，也不要太松。When bandaging, don't make it too tight or too loose.
>   *Bāozā shí jì búyào tài jǐn, yě búyào tài sōng.*
> 3. 止血方法既有指压法，也有加压包扎法。The hemostasis strategies include both finger-pressing manipulation and pressure dressing.
>   *Zhǐxiě fāngfǎ jì yǒu zhǐyāfǎ, yě yǒu jiāyā bāozāfǎ.*

语法练习 1 Grammar Exercise 1

用"既……也……"改写句子。Rewrite the sentences with "既 ... 也 ...".

1. 包扎时，不要太紧、太松。

_____

183

❷ 止血方法可以用指压法、加压包扎法或止血带止血法。
_____

❸ 悬吊包扎可以使用绷带、三角巾。
_____

❹ 没有呼吸和心跳，也没有意识的病人，采取仰卧位。
_____

语法点 2 Grammar Point 2

指示代词：这样　Demonstrative pronoun: 这样

代词"这样"指示性质、状态、方式、程度等。

The pronoun "这样" indicates nature, state, manner, degree, etc.

例句：
❶ 包扎时应该抬高患肢，这样可以减轻肿胀。When dressing, the affected limb should be raised to alleviate swelling.
（Bāozā shí yīnggāi táigāo huànzhī, zhèyàng kěyǐ jiǎnqīng zhǒngzhàng.）

❷ 你这样包扎，太紧，应该放松。Your dressing is too tight. You should loosen it.
（Nǐ zhèyàng bāozā, tài jǐn, yīnggāi fàngsōng.）

❸ 可以用三角巾固定，这样效果更好。It can be fixed with a triangular bandage, which works better.
（Kěyǐ yòng sānjiǎojīn gùdìng, zhèyàng xiàoguǒ gèng hǎo.）

语法练习 2 Grammar Exercise 2

把"这样"放在句中合适的位置。Put "这样" in the right place in the sentence.

❶ ____你____包扎，太紧，____应该放松____。

2. 可以____用三角巾固定____，____效果____更好。

3. 包扎时____应该抬高患肢____，____可以减轻____肿胀。

4. 活动性____出血____的病人，要____治疗。

汉字书写 Writing Chinese Characters

yuán
元 元元元元
元 元元元元

wán
完 完完完完完完
完 完完完完

yuǎn
远 远远远远远远远
远 远远远远

yuàn
院 院院院院院院院院院
院 院院院院

文化拓展 Culture Insight

One of the Four Great Inventions of Ancient China: Papermaking

By the Western Han Dynasty (202–9 BC), the basic principles of papermaking were already understood. During the Eastern Han Dynasty (25–220 AD), Cai Lun, a court eunuch, refined the papermaking process by using plant fibers such as bark, hemp, rags, and old fishing nets as raw materials. This innovation significantly improved the quality of paper. Paper gradually replaced bamboo and silk as a more widely accessible writing material, facilitating the circulation of texts and knowledge. Chinese papermaking technology had a lasting impact on the development of the world's papermaking industry and contributed greatly to the dissemination of human civilization.

小结 Summary

词语 Words

朗读词语。 Read the words aloud.

绷带	三角巾	固定
肿胀	血液	苍白—青紫

语法 Grammar

朗读句子。 Read the sentences aloud.

1. 悬吊包扎既使用绷带，也使用三角巾。
2. 外伤包扎既可以用绷带包扎，也可以用三角巾包扎。

3 包扎时应该抬高患肢,这样可以减轻肿胀。

4 包扎时要松紧适宜,这样不会影响血液循环。

课文理解 Text Comprehension

根据课文内容选词填空。Fill in the blanks with correct words according to the text.

A 抬高　　B 松紧　　C 绷带　　D 固定　　E 三角巾包扎

外伤包扎的方法有绷带包扎、_____和悬吊包扎。悬吊包扎使用_____和三角巾,三角巾的_____效果更好。包扎时应该_____患肢,这样可以减轻肿胀。包扎时要_____适宜,这样不会影响血液循环。

第20课 Lesson 20

Sìzhī bēngdài bāozā
四肢绷带包扎
Limb Bandaging

复习 Revision

朗读句子。Read the sentences aloud.

1. 悬吊包扎既使用绷带，也使用三角巾。
2. 三角巾固定效果更好。
3. 包扎时应该抬高患肢，这样可以减轻肿胀。
4. 病人手指苍白或青紫，说明包扎太紧。

热身 Warming Up

看图选词。Look at the pictures and choose the correct words.

A 胶布 jiāobù tape
B 纱布 shābù gauze
C 伤口 shāngkǒu wound
D 肘部 zhǒubù elbow

188

第 20 课 | 四肢绷带包扎

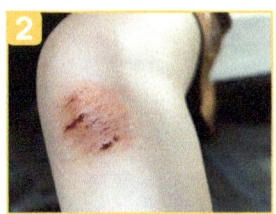

学习生词 Words and Expressions 20-1

1	螺旋	luóxuán	n.	spiral
2	常	cháng	adv.	commonly
3	弹力绷带	tánlì bēngdài		elastic bandage
4	前臂	qiánbì	n.	forearm
5	无菌纱布	wújūn shābù		sterile gauze
6	覆盖	fùgài	v.	cover
7	伤口	shāngkǒu	n.	wound
8	腕部	wànbù	n.	wrist
9	环形	huánxíng	n.	loop
10	圈	quān	n.	circle
11	斜行	xié xíng		diagonally
13	压	yā	v.	press
14	肘部	zhǒubù	n.	elbow
15	胶布	jiāobù	n.	tape
16	露	lù	v.	expose

189

词语练习 Words Exercises

1. 看图说词。Look at the pictures and say the words.

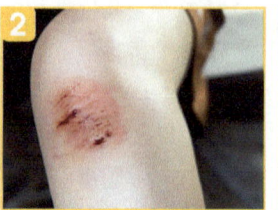

2. 朗读词语搭配。Read the collocations aloud.

弹力绷带

无菌纱布

环形缠绕

露出手指

学习课文 Text 🎧 20-2

Sìzhī bēngdài bāozā
四肢绷带包扎

Sìzhī wàishāng cǎiqǔ luóxuán bāozāfǎ. Cháng yòng tánlì bēngdài
四肢外伤采取螺旋包扎法。常用弹力绷带
jìnxíng bāozā. Yǐ qiánbì wéi lì:
进行包扎。以前臂为例：

Yòng wújūn shābù fùgài shāngkǒu.
1. 用无菌纱布覆盖伤口。

Yòng bēngdài zài wànbù huánxíng chánrào èr zhī sān quān, zài xié
2. 用绷带在腕部环形缠绕2—3圈，再斜行向上缠绕，每一圈压在上一圈的 1/2 处，在肘部环形包扎结束。用胶布固定绷带。

3. 包扎要松紧适宜。露出手指。评估病人的血液循环情况。

Limb Bandaging

Spiral bandaging is used for limb injuries. Elastic bandages are commonly used for wrapping. Taking the forearm as an example:

1. Cover the wound with sterile gauze.

2. Circularly wrap a bandage around the wrist for 2–3 times. Then wrap diagonally upwards, pressing each lap on half of the previous lap. End the circular bandaging at the elbow. Fix the bandage with a tape.

3. The tightness of the wrapping should be appropriate. Expose the fingers. Assess the blood circulation of the patient.

课文练习 Text Exercises

1. 判断正误。True or false.

① 四肢外伤采取螺旋包扎法。

② 常用三角巾进行包扎。

❸ 在腕部环形包扎结束。

❹ 四肢外伤包扎时要露出手指。

2. 选词填空。 Fill in the blanks with the correct words.

| A 1/2 | B 循环 | C 弹力绷带 | D 无菌纱布 |

❶ 四肢外伤采取螺旋包扎法。常用_____进行包扎。

❷ 用_____覆盖伤口。

❸ 向上缠绕，每一圈压在上一圈的_____处。

❹ 露出手指，评估血液_____情况。

学习语法 Grammar

语法点 1 Grammar Point 1

名词作状语 Using Nouns as Adverbials

名词除了可以作主语、定语和宾语外，有时还可以作状语，表示动作的方式。

In addition to being the subject, attributive, and object, nouns can sometimes also be used as adverbials to indicate actions.

例句：
❶ 用绷带在腕部环形缠绕 2 — 3 圈。Circularly wrap a bandage around the wrist for 2–3 times.
Yòng bēngdài zài wànbù huánxíng chánrào èr zhì sān quān.

❷ 环形包扎 10 圈。Circularly wrap for 10 times.
Huánxíng bāozā shí quān.

❸ 8 字（figure）包扎手部。Wrap the hand in the shape of 8.
Bā zì bāozā shǒubù.

语法练习 1 Grammar Exercise 1

按照正确的语序连词成句。Make sentences in correct orders with the given words or phrases.

1. ①用绷带　②在腕部　③环形　④缠绕2—3圈

_____

2. ①8字　②包扎　③手部

_____

3. ①环形　②包扎　③10圈

_____

4. ①可以　②用于四肢　③包扎　④绷带

_____

语法点 2 Grammar Point 2

补语：数量补语　Complement: the complement of quantity

数量补语：动词＋动量补语。动量补语由数词与动量词构成，用来说明动作的次数。

The complement of quantity: verb + complement of frequency. The complement of frequency is composed of a numeral and an action measure word, which indicates the frequency of the action.

例句：
1. 用绷带在腕部环形缠绕 2 — 3 圈。Circularly wrap a bandage around the wrist for 2–3 times.
2. 在肘部环形包扎 2 圈。Circularly wrap the elbow for 2 times.
3. 斜行向上缠绕 1/2 圈。Wrap diagonally upwards for one and a half times.

语法练习 2 Grammar Exercise 2

按照正确的语序连词成句。Make sentences in correct orders with the given words or phrases.

1. ①圈　②包扎　③2—3　④环形
   _____

2. ①在　②腕部　③2—3 圈　④缠绕
   _____

3. ①缠绕　②向上　③2—3　④圈
   _____

4. ①用　②包扎　③绷带　④2—3 圈
   _____

汉字书写 Writing Chinese Characters

bù
不　不 不 不 不

cái
才　才 才 才 才

hái
还　还 还 还 还 还 还

第 20 课 | 四肢绷带包扎

bēi 杯杯杯杯杯杯杯杯
杯 杯 杯 杯 杯

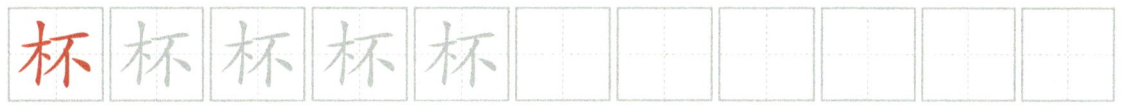

职业拓展 Career Insight

The Emblem on the Ambulance

In China, the emergency phone number is 120. Alongside the "Red Cross" symbol, ambulances often display another symbol known as the "Star of Life," the international emblem of the Emergency Medical Service System (EMS). The Star of Life appears on ambulances, helicopters, medical equipment, and uniforms of EMS personnel. In Western medicine, the "snake coiled around a staff" is a common medical symbol. The staff represents the healer's journey to treat illnesses, while the snake symbolizes health and longevity.

小结 Summary

词语 Words

朗读词语。Read the words aloud.

| 螺旋包扎 | 弹力绷带 | 无菌纱布 | 覆盖伤口 |
| 前臂 | 腕部 | 肘部 | 环形 |

195

语法 Grammar

朗读句子。Read the sentences aloud.

1. 对四肢外伤采取螺旋包扎。
2. 用绷带在腕部环形缠绕 2—3 圈。
3. 每一圈压在上一圈的 1/2 处。
4. 对每个病人，医生都要先评估病情。

课文理解 Text Comprehension

选词填空，说明用绷带包扎前臂的方法。Fill in the blanks with the correct words, and explain the method of limb bandaging.

A 环形包扎	B 血液循环	C 无菌纱布
D 弹力绷带	E 2—3 圈	F 1/2 处

1. 前臂受伤，用_____包扎。
2. 用_____覆盖伤口。
3. 用绷带在腕部环形缠绕_____。再斜行向上缠绕，每一圈压在上一圈的_____。在肘部_____结束。用胶布固定。
4. 包扎松紧适宜，露出手指。评估_____情况。

第21课 Lesson 21

手部绷带包扎
Shǒubù bēngdài bāozā
Hand Bandaging

复习 Revision

朗读句子。Read the sentences aloud.

1. 四肢外伤采取螺旋包扎法。
2. 常用弹力绷带进行包扎。
3. 用绷带在腕部环形缠绕 2—3 圈。
4. 每一圈压在上一圈的 1/2 处。

热身 Warming Up

看图选词。Look at the pictures and choose the correct words.

A 锁骨 (suǒgǔ) clavicle　　B 形状 (xíngzhuàng) shape
C 骨折 (gǔzhé) fracture　　D 关节 (guānjié) joint

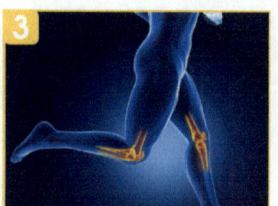

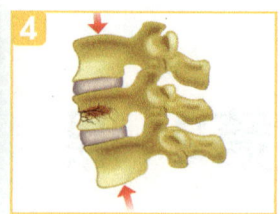

学习生词 Words and Expressions 🎧 21-1

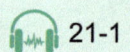

1	字	zì	*n.*	figure
2	形状	xíngzhuàng	*n.*	shape
3	像	xiàng	*v.*	resemble
4	主要	zhǔyào	*adj.*	main
5	于	yú	*prep.*	in; at; on
6	关节	guānjié	*n.*	joint
7	锁骨	suǒgǔ	*n.*	clavicle
8	骨折	gǔzhé	*v.*	fracture
9	操作	cāozuò	*v.*	operate
10	从	cóng	*prep.*	from
11	外	wài	*n.*	outside
12	远端	yuǎnduān	*n.*	far end
13	然后	ránhòu	*conj.*	then
14	近端	jìnduān	*n.*	proximal end

第 21 课 | 手部绷带包扎

词语练习 Words Exercises

1. 看图说词。Look at the pictures and say the words.

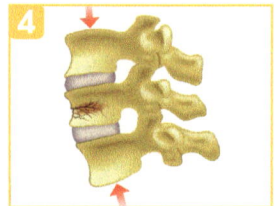

2. 朗读短语。Read the phrases aloud.

- 8 字包扎
- 从内向外
- 锁骨骨折
- 远端 — 近端

学习课文 Text 🎧 21-2

Shǒubù bēngdài bāozā
手部绷带包扎

Shǒubù wàishāng cǎiqǔ bā zì bāozāfǎ（yīnwèi xíngzhuàng xiàng bā zì）。Zhèzhǒng bāozā fāngfǎ zhǔyào yòngyú guānjié de wàishāng bāozā、suǒgǔ gǔzhé de gùdìng。Cāozuò fāngfǎ rúxià:

手部外伤采取 8 字包扎法（因为 形状 像 8 字）。这种 包扎方法主要用于关节的外伤包扎、锁骨骨折的固定。操作方法如下：

199

1. 打开无菌纱布，包扎伤口。

2. 打开弹力绷带，在腕部从内向外缠绕两圈。

3. 斜行向远端，在四指缠绕1圈。然后斜行向近端，在腕部缠绕1圈。

4. 连续做8字包扎。

Hand Bandaging

Hand injuries are treated with the 8-shape bandaging (as it resembles the shape of 8). This bandaging method is mainly used for joint trauma bandaging and fixation for clavicle fractures. The operating method is as follows:

1. Open a sterile gauze and cover the wound.

2. Open the elastic bandage and wrap it twice around the wrist from inside to outside.

3. Wrap diagonally towards the far end and wrap one circle around the four fingers. Then move diagonally towards the proximal end and wrap it around the wrist for one circle.

4. Perform continuous 8-shape bandaging.

第 21 课 | 手部绷带包扎

课文练习 Text Exercises

1. 判断正误。True or false.

① 叫（jiào, call）8 字包扎法，是因为形状像 8 字。

② 8 字包扎法只用于固定锁骨骨折。

③ 在腕部从内向外缠绕两圈。

④ 然后斜行向远端在四指缠绕。

2. 选词填空。Fill in the blanks with the correct words.

① 手部外伤采取_____包扎法。

　A 环形　　　　　B 8 字　　　　　C 螺旋形

② 这种包扎方法主要用于_____的外伤包扎。

　A 关节　　　　　B 上臂　　　　　C 小臂

③ 在腕部_____缠绕两圈。

　A 从内向外　　　B 从外向内　　　C 从前向后

④ _____做 8 字包扎。

　A 继续　　　　　B 连续　　　　　C 主要

学习语法 Grammar

语法点 1 Grammar Point 1

介词：于　Preposition: 于

介词"于"放在动词后，可以表示方面、原因、目的。

The preposition "于" can be used after a verb to indicate the aspect, reason and purpose.

201

例句：

1. Bā zì bāozāfǎ zhǔyào yòngyú guānjié de wàishāng bāozā, suǒgǔ gǔzhé de gùdìng.
8字包扎法主要用于关节的外伤包扎、锁骨骨折的固定。The 8-shape bandaging is mainly used for joint trauma bandaging and fixation for clavicle fractures.

2. Zhǐxiědài zhǐxiěfǎ yòngyú sìzhī dàdòngmài de zhǐxiě.
止血带止血法用于四肢大动脉的止血。The hemostasis with tourniquet is used to stop bleeding of the large arteries of the limbs.

3. Sānjiǎojīn kěyǐ yòngyú bāozā wàishāng.
三角巾可以用于包扎外伤。Triangle bandages can be used to bandage external injuries.

语法练习 1 Grammar Exercise 1

连线组句。Draw lines to make sentences.

止血带止血法 •		• 关节外伤包扎
三角巾 •	• 用于 •	• 四肢大动脉止血
8字包扎法 •		• 包扎外伤
		• 固定锁骨骨折

语法点 2 Grammar Point 2

介词：从 Preposition: 从

介词"从"表示时间、处所的起点。结构"从……向……+动词"可以表示动作的起点和朝向。
The preposition "从" indicates the starting point in time or location. The structure "从…向…+ verb" can indicate the starting point and direction of the action.

例句：
1. 在腕部从内向外缠绕两圈。Wrap the wrist twice from the inside out.
2. 救护车从病人家里向医院开（drive）。The ambulance drives from the patient's home to the hospital.
3. 上肢绷带包扎方法是，从腕部向肘部环形包扎。The method of upper limb bandaging is to circularly wrap it from the wrist to the elbow.

语法练习 2 Grammar Exercise 2

用"从……向……"完成句子。Complete the sentences with "从 ... 向 ...".

1. 在腕部_____（外　　内）缠绕两圈。
2. 斜行向远端缠绕 1 圈，然后再斜行_____（远端　　近端）缠绕 1 圈。
3. 救护车_____（病人家里　　医院）开。
4. 上肢外伤，用绷带_____（腕部　　肘部）环形包扎。

汉字书写 Writing Chinese Characters

mù 木　木 木 木 木

shù 术 术 术 术 术 术

lín 林 林 林 林 林 林 林 林 林

chuáng 床 床 床 床 床 床 床 床

文化拓展 Culture Insight

One of the Four Great Inventions of Ancient China: Movable Type Printing

The earliest known printing technique, the rubbing technique, was developed during the reign of Emperor Ling of the Eastern Han Dynasty (157–189). This method used paper to transfer texts and images from stone tablets or other objects. Later, during the Tang Dynasty (618–907), woodblock printing was invented, involving carved images and texts on blocks for printing. In the Song Dynasty (960–1279), Bi Sheng, during Emperor Renzong's reign (1010–1063), invented movable type printing, which allowed individual characters to be rearranged for printing. This method was flexible, time-saving, and labor-saving. Printing technology later spread to Korea, Japan, Central Asia, West Asia, and Europe, laying the groundwork for modern civilization by enabling the widespread dissemination and exchange of knowledge.

第 21 课 | 手部绷带包扎

小结 Summary

词语 Words

朗读词语。Read the words aloud.

| 形状 | 关节 | 锁骨 | 骨折 | 远端 | 近端 |

语法 Grammar

朗读句子。Read the sentences aloud.

1. 这种包扎方法主要用于关节的外伤包扎、锁骨骨折的固定。
2. 8 字包扎法用于手部外伤包扎。
3. 在腕部从内向外缠绕两圈。
4. 斜行从远端向近端在腕部缠绕 1 圈。

课文理解 Text Comprehension

根据课文内容给下列句子排序。Put the statements in the correct order according to the text.

1. 用弹力绷带在腕部从内向外缠绕两圈。
2. 打开无菌纱布，包扎伤口。
3. 连续做 8 字包扎。
4. 斜行向远端，在四指缠绕 1 圈。然后斜行向近端，在腕部缠绕 1 圈。

第22课 膝部绷带包扎
Lesson 22　Knee Bandaging

Xībù　bēngdài　bāozā

复习 Revision

选词填空。Fill in the blanks with the correct words.

1. 手部外伤采取8_____包扎法。

   A 字　　　　B 形　　　　C 状

2. 这种包扎方法可以用于_____的外伤包扎。

   A 腕部　　　B 关节　　　C 锁骨

3. 8字包扎法用于关节的外伤包扎和锁骨_____的固定。

   A 进入　　　B 骨折　　　C 打开

4. 在腕部从_____向内缠绕两圈。

   A 外　　　　B 远端　　　C 近端

第 22 课 | 膝部绷带包扎

热身 Warming Up

将图片和对应词语连线。Match the pictures with the corresponding words.

1 •   • 膝关节 xīguānjié knee joint

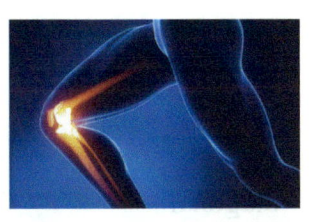

2 •   • 弯曲 wānqū curve

3 •   • 敷料 fūliào dressing

4 •   • 方向 fāngxiàng direction

学习生词 Words and Expressions 22-1

| 1 | 膝 | xī | n. | knee |
| 2 | 跟……一样 | gēn...yíyàng | | the same as... |

3	弯曲	wānqū	*adj.*	curve
4	成	chéng	*v.*	become
5	度	dù	*measure word*	degree
6	敷料	fūliào	*n.*	dressing
7	沿	yán	*prep.*	along
8	对角	duìjiǎo		diagonal
9	方向	fāngxiàng	*n.*	direction
10	下	xià	*n.*	downwards
11	至	zhì	*v.*	to
12	下方	xiàfāng	*n.*	below
13	上方	shàngfāng	*n.*	upper
14	重复	chóngfù	*v.*	repeat
15	直到	zhídào	*v.*	until
16	完全	wánquán	*adv.*	completely
17	住	zhù	*v.*	(used as a complement after a verb to indicate a steadiness or firmness)

词语练习　Words Exercises

1. 看图说词。Look at the pictures and say the words.

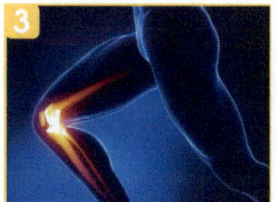

2. 朗读词语搭配。Read the collocations aloud.

- 包扎膝部
- 弯曲膝关节
- 固定敷料
- 沿对角方向
- 重复进行

学习课文 Text 🎧 22-2

膝部绷带包扎
Xībù bēngdài bāozā

膝部的包扎方法跟手部一样，也用8字包扎法。

1. 把病人的膝关节弯曲成90度。用绷带在关节处缠绕2—3圈，固定敷料。

2. 沿对角方向斜行向下缠绕至关节下方。

3. 再沿对角方向斜行向上缠绕至关节上方。

4. 重复进行8字缠绕，直到膝关节完全包扎。每圈绷带压住上一圈的一半。

Knee Bandaging

The way of knee bandaging is the same as that of the hands, using the 8-shape bandaging.

1. Bend the patient's knee joint to 90 degrees. Use the bandage to wrap 2–3 circles around the joint to fix the dressing.
2. Wrap diagonally downward to below the joint.
3. Wrap diagonally upward to above the joint.
4. Repeat the 8-shape wrapping process until the joint is completely wrapped. Overlap each wrap by half of the previous layer.

课文练习 Text Exercises

1. 判断正误。True or false.

1. 膝部的包扎方法跟手部不一样。
2. 用绷带在关节处缠绕2—3圈，固定敷料。
3. 沿对角方向斜行向下和向上缠绕。
4. 每圈压住上一圈的1/2。

2. 选词填空。Fill in the blanks with the correct words.

1. 膝部的包扎方法跟手部一样，也用_____包扎法。

    A 螺旋　　　　B 8字　　　　C 对角

2. 把病人的膝关节_____成90度。

    A 方向　　　　B 弯曲　　　　C 伸出

第 22 课 | 膝部绷带包扎

3 沿_____方向斜行向下缠绕至关节下方。

A 对角　　　　B 三角　　　　C 环形

4 每圈压住上一圈的_____。

A 一半　　　　B 所有　　　　C 重要

学习语法 Grammar

语法点 1　Grammar Point 1

比较句：A 跟 B 一样 / 不一样　　The comparative sentence: A 跟 B 一样 / 不一样

表示 A、B 在某方面有相同或不同之处。

It indicates that A and B have similarities or differences in a certain aspect.

例句：

1 　　　Xībù de bāozā fāngfǎ gēn shǒubù yíyàng, yě yòng bā zì bāozāfǎ.
膝部的包扎方法跟手部一样，也用 8 字包扎法。The way of knee bandaging is the same as that of the hands, using the 8-shape bandaging.

2 　　　Gēn cèliáng tǐwēn yíyàng, cèliáng xuèyā qián, bìngrén yào xiūxi sānshí fēnzhōng.
跟测量体温一样，测量血压前，病人要休息 30 分钟。Just like measuring the body temperature, patients need to rest for 30 minutes before measuring blood pressure.

3 　　　Gēn yǐqián bù yíyàng, zhè cì wǒ duì zhè zhǒng yàowù guòmǐn.
跟以前不一样，这次我对这种药物过敏。Unlike before, this time I am allergic to this medication.

语法练习 1　Grammar Exercise 1

用 "A 跟 B 一样" 完成句子。Complete the sentences with "A 跟 B 一样".

1. _____（测量血压　测量体温），测量前病人要休息 30 分钟。

2. _____（我　他），也对这种药物过敏。

3. _____（膝部包扎　手部包扎），也用 8 字包扎法。

4. _____（前臂包扎　膝部包扎），每一圈也要压在上一圈的 1/2 处。

语法点 2　Grammar Point 2

介词：沿　Preposition: 沿

介词"沿"表示顺着某个方向或路径。
The preposition "沿" indicates following a direction or path.

例句：
1. 沿对角方向斜行向下缠绕至关节下方。Wrap diagonally downward to below the joint.
2. 再沿对角方向斜行向上缠绕至关节上方。Wrap diagonally upward to above the joint.
3. 救护车沿这条（measure word for roads）路（road）赶到病人的家。The ambulance rushed to the patient's home along the road.

第 22 课 ｜ 膝部绷带包扎

语法练习 2 Grammar Exercise 2

把"沿"放在句中合适的位置。Put "沿" in the right place in the sentence.

1. ____对角方向____斜行向下____缠绕____至关节下方。
2. ____这条路____向前____开 1 分钟____就是病人家。
3. ____这条通道（tōngdào, passage）____往前走____就是____观察室。
4. ____血____手指____流下（liúxià, flow down）____。

汉字书写 Writing Chinese Characters

rì	日 日 日 日
日	日 日 日 日

bái	白 白 白 白 白
白	白 白 白 白

yuè	月 月 月 月
月	月 月 月 月

míng	明 明 明 明 明 明 明
明	明 明 明 明

职业拓展 Career Insight

Nightingale's Oath

I solemnly pledge myself before God and in the presence of this assembly to live my life in purity and to practice my profession faithfully. I will abstain from all that is deleterious and mischievous and will neither take nor knowingly administer any harmful drug. I will do all in my power to maintain and elevate the standards of my profession and will hold in confidence all personal matters entrusted to me and all family affairs that come to my knowledge in the practice of my calling. With loyalty, I will endeavor to aid the physician in his work and devote myself to the welfare of those committed to my care.

—— *The Florence Nightingale Pledge*

小结 Summary

词语 Words

朗读词语。Read the words aloud.

膝关节	弯曲	对角
敷料	重复	方向

第 22 课 | 膝部绷带包扎

语法 Grammar

朗读句子。Read the sentences aloud.

1. 膝部的包扎方法跟手部一样。
2. 沿对角方向斜行向下缠绕至关节下方。
3. 再沿对角方向斜行向上缠绕至关节上方。
4. 跟他一样,我也对这种药物过敏。

课文理解 Text Comprehension

根据课文内容给下列句子排序。Put the statements in the correct order according to the text.

1. 重复进行 8 字缠绕。
2. 沿对角方向斜行向下缠绕至关节下方。
3. 膝关节弯曲成 90 度。用绷带在关节处缠绕 2—3 圈,固定敷料。
4. 再沿对角方向斜行向上缠绕至关节上方。

第23课 Lesson 23

踝部绷带包扎
Huáibù bēngdài bāozā
Ankle Bandaging

复习 Revision

填写正确的答案。Fill in the blanks with the correct answers.

1. 膝部包扎用_____法。
2. 包扎膝部时，膝关节弯曲成_____度。
3. 绷带沿_____方向斜行向下和向上缠绕。
4. 绷带每圈要压住上一圈的_____。

热身 Warming Up

看图选词。Look at the pictures and choose the correct words.

A 踝部 huáibù ankle
B 坐 zuò sit
C 患处 huànchù affected area
D 冷敷 lěngfū cold compress

第 23 课 ｜ 踝部绷带包扎

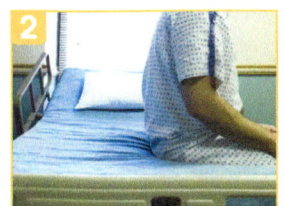

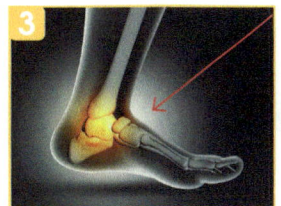

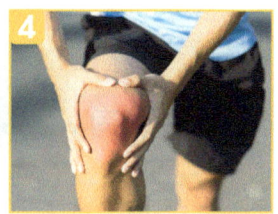

学习生词 Words and Expressions 🎧 23-1

1	踝部	huáibù	n.	ankle
2	比	bǐ	prep.	than
3	难	nán	adj.	difficult
4	一些	yìxiē		some
5	处理	chǔlǐ	v.	treat
6	让	ràng	v.	let
7	坐	zuò	v.	sit
8	下来	xiàlái	v.	get down
9	冰袋	bīngdài	n.	ice pack
10	冷敷	lěngfū	v.	cold compress
11	如果	rúguǒ	conj.	if
12	剧烈	jùliè	adj.	severe
13	缓解	huǎnjiě	v.	relieve
14	送	sòng	v.	send
15	去	qù	v.	go to

217

急救护理（基里巴斯版） 初级篇

词语练习 Words Exercises

1. 看图说词。Look at the pictures and say the words.

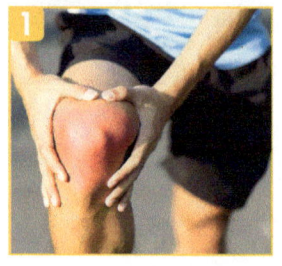

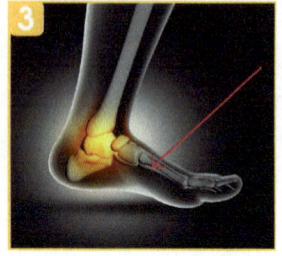

2. 朗读词语搭配。Read the collocations aloud.

- 踝部扭伤
- 踝部出血
- 踝部骨折
- 处理措施
- 坐下来休息
- 使用冰袋冷敷
- 用绷带包扎

学习课文 Text 🎧 23-2

Huáibù bēngdài bāozā
踝部绷带包扎

Huáibù bāozā bǐ xībù bāozā nán yìxiē yě yòng bā zì
踝部包扎比膝部包扎难一些，也用8字

bāozāfǎ. Huáibù niǔshāng, chūxiě huò gǔzhé chǔlǐ cuòshī rúxià:
包扎法。踝部扭伤、出血或骨折处理措施如下：

Ràng bìngrén zuò xiàlái xiūxi.
1. 让 病人坐下来休息。

Táigāo huànzhī.
2. 抬高 患肢。

218

第 23 课 ｜ 踝部绷带包扎

3. 使用冰袋冷敷踝部。
4. 用绷带包扎踝部。

如果病人疼痛剧烈，不能缓解，可能是骨折，应该尽快送病人去医院。

Ankle Bandaging

Ankle bandaging is more difficult than knee bandaging, and also uses the 8-shape bandaging. The treatment measures for ankle sprains, bleeding, or fractures are as follows:

1. Let the patient sit and rest.
2. Raise the affected limb.
3. Apply an ice pack to the ankle for a cold compress.
4. Wrap the ankle with a bandage.

If the patient experiences a severe and unrelieved pain, it may indicate a fracture, and they should be sent to the hospital as soon as possible.

课文练习 Text Exercises

1. 判断正误。True or false.

1. 踝部包扎不用 8 字包扎法。
2. 踝部扭伤应该先冷敷。

③ 踝部疼痛剧烈，不能缓解，可能是骨折。

④ 骨折病人应该尽快在病人家里治疗。

2. 选词填空。Fill in the blanks with the correct words.

① 踝部包扎_____一些。

    A 难　　　　　B 剧烈　　　　　C 高

② 踝部扭伤、出血或骨折的_____步骤有4个。

    A 冷敷　　　　B 处理　　　　　C 尽快

③ 使用冰袋_____踝部。

    A 治疗　　　　B 抬高　　　　　C 冷敷

④ 踝部病人冷敷、包扎后，疼痛不缓解，可能是_____。

    A 骨折　　　　B 扭伤　　　　　C 出血

学习语法 Grammar

语法点 1　Grammar Point 1

比较句：A 比 B ＋ 形容词 ＋ 数量补语　Comparative sentence: A 比 B + adjective + complement of quantity

"A 比 B ＋形容词" 表示 A 和 B 比较后，A 在程度上更高。"A 比 B ＋形容词＋数量补语" 表示 A 在程度上高于 B 的数量。

"A比B + adjective" indicates that after comparing A and B, A has a higher degree. "A比B + adjective + complement of quantity" indicates the specific degree that A is higher than B.

例句：
1. 踝部包扎比膝部包扎难一些。Ankle bandaging is more difficult than knee bandaging.
2. 他的体温比正常体温高1度。His body temperature is one degree higher than normal.
3. 这种疼痛，今天（today）比昨天（yesterday）多两次。This kind of pain occurred twice as often today as it did yesterday.

语法练习 1 Grammar Exercise 1

按照正确的语序连词成句。Make sentences in correct orders with the given words or phrases.

1. ①膝部包扎　②踝部包扎　③比　④一些　⑤难

　_____

2. ①他的体温　②正常体温　③比　④高　⑤1度

　_____

3. ①三角巾包扎的固定效果　②绷带包扎　③比　④好　⑤一些

　_____

4. ①扭伤　②骨折的疼痛　③比　④剧烈　⑤一些

　_____

语法点 2 Grammar Point 2

特殊句型：兼语句 Special sentence pattern: the pivotal sentence

"主语＋使／叫／让／请／送＋宾语 1＋动词＋宾语 2"是兼语句的基本形式。宾语 1 既是第一个动词的宾语，同时在语义上又是第二个动词的主语。

The basic form of a pivotal sentence is "subject ＋ 使／叫／让／请／送 ＋ object 1 ＋ verb ＋ object 2". The object 1 is both the object of the first verb and the semantic subject of the second verb.

例句：

1. Hùshi ràng bìngrén zuò xiàlái xiūxi.
   护士让病人坐下来休息。The nurse asked the patient to sit and rest.

2. Yīshēng sòng gǔzhé bìngrén qù yīyuàn.
   医生送骨折病人去医院。The doctor sent the fractured patient to the hospital.

3. Hùshi bú ràng bìngrén xīyān.
   护士不让病人吸烟（smoke）。Nurses do not allow the patient to smoke.

语法练习 2 Grammar Exercise 2

用兼语句改写下列句子。Rewrite the sentences with the pivotal sentece pattern.

1. 护士告诉（gàosù，tell）病人　　病人坐下来休息

   _____

2. 医生告诉病人　　病人抬高患肢

   _____

3. 护士告诉病人　　病人膝部弯曲成 90 度

   _____

4 病人打电话叫救护车　　救护车赶到病人家里

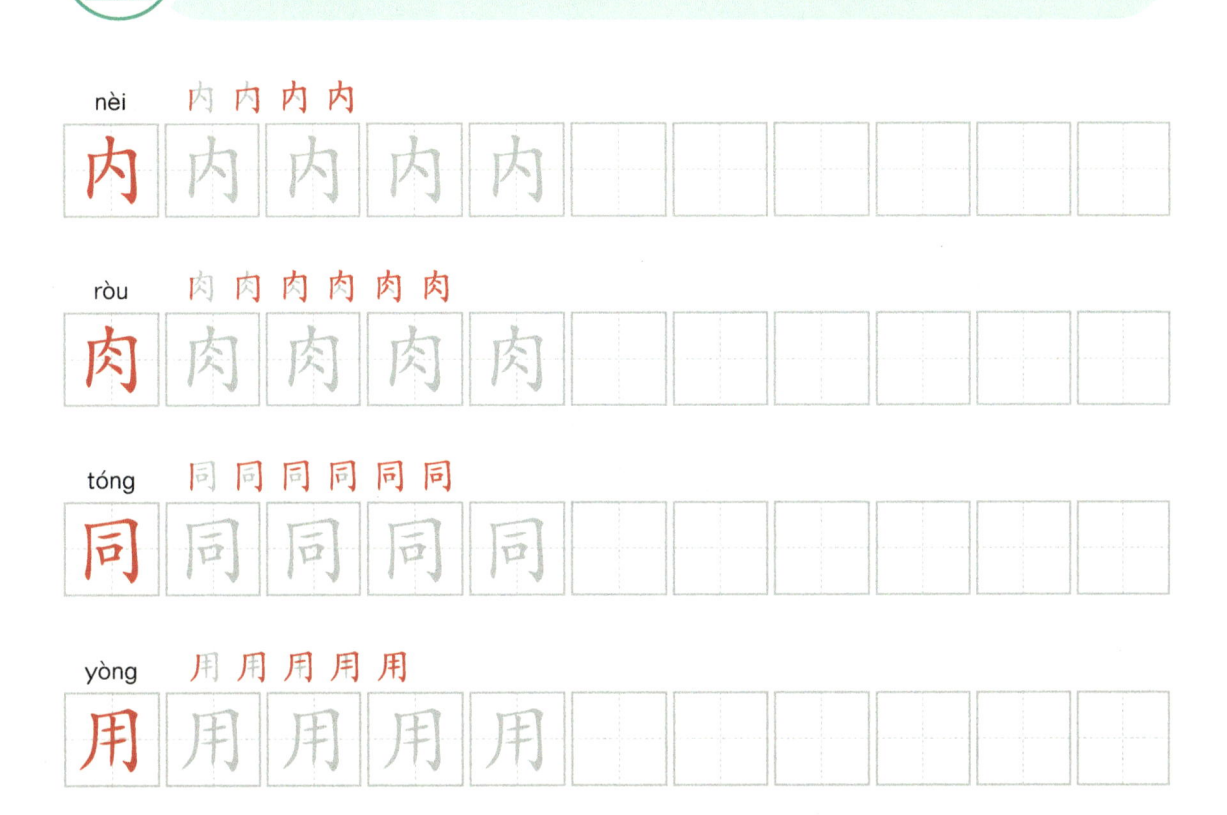

汉字书写 Writing Chinese Characters

nèi
内　内 内 内 内
　　内 内 内 内

ròu
肉　肉 肉 肉 肉 肉
　　肉 肉 肉 肉

tóng
同　同 同 同 同 同
　　同 同 同 同

yòng
用　用 用 用 用
　　用 用 用 用

文化拓展 Culture Insight

One of the Four Great Inventions of Ancient China: Gunpowder

The invention of gunpowder originated from the ancient Chinese people's long-standing practices in alchemy and medicine, with a history of over a thousand years. By the end of the Tang Dynasty (618–907), gunpowder was being used for military purposes. In the 12th and 13th centuries, it was introduced to Arab countries and subsequently spread to Greece, Europe, and other parts of the world.

小结 Summary

词语 Words

朗读词语。Read the words aloud.

踝部	处理	冰袋
冷敷	剧烈	缓解

语法 Grammar

朗读句子。Read the sentences aloud.

1. 踝部包扎比膝部包扎难一些。
2. 骨折比扭伤痛一些。
3. 护士让病人坐下来休息。
4. 医生让病人抬高患肢。

第 23 课 | 踝部绷带包扎

课文理解 Text Comprehension

根据课文内容给下列句子排序。Put the statements in the correct order according to the text.

1. 使用冰袋冷敷踝部。
2. 用绷带包扎踝部。
3. 让病人坐下来休息。
4. 抬高患肢。
5. 疼痛不缓解,可能是骨折,尽快送医院。

第24课 Lesson 24

Sānjiǎojīn xuándiào bāozā
三角巾悬吊包扎
Triangle Bandage Suspension

复习 Revision

朗读句子。Read the sentences aloud.

1. 踝部包扎比膝部包扎难一些。
2. 踝部扭伤、出血或骨折用8字包扎法。
3. 让病人坐下来休息。
4. 使用冰袋冷敷踝部。

热身 Warming Up

看图选词。Look at the pictures and choose the correct words.

A 肩(jiān) shoulder   B 左(zuǒ) left — 右(yòu) right
C 急救箱(jíjiùxiāng) first-aid kit   D 肘(zhǒu) elbow

226

第 24 课 | 三角巾悬吊包扎

学习生词 Words and Expressions 24-1

1	经常	jīngcháng	adv.	often
2	急救箱	jíjiùxiāng	n.	first-aid kit
3	中	zhōng	n.	inside
4	见到	jiàndào		see
5	肩	jiān	n.	shoulder
6	伤员	shāngyuán	n.	injured person
7	屈	qū	v.	bend
8	肘	zhǒu	n.	elbow
9	身上	shēnshàng	n.	body
10	铺	pū	v.	spread

227

11	开	kāi	v.	open
12	底角	dǐjiǎo	n.	base angle
13	搭	dā	v.	rest on
14	左	zuǒ	n.	left
15	顶角	dǐngjiǎo	n.	vertex angle
16	则	zé	conj.	(used to indicate contrast)
17	包裹	bāoguǒ	n.	wrap
18	脖子	bózi	n.	neck

词语练习 Words Exercises

1. 看图说词。 Look at the pictures and say the words.

2. 朗读词语搭配。 Read the collocations aloud.

肩部外伤　　锁骨外伤　　上肢外伤

屈肘90度　　包裹前臂　　悬吊包扎

学习课文 Text 🎧 24-2

三角巾悬吊包扎

三角巾经常可以在急救箱中见到。三角巾悬吊包扎法适用于肩部、锁骨或上肢外伤。操作方法如下：

1. 伤员屈肘90度，手掌向内。
2. 把三角巾在伤员身上铺开，两个底角搭在左、右肩上，顶角则放在肘下，包裹住前臂。
3. 两个底角打活结，把三角巾悬吊在伤员脖子上。

Triangle Bandage Suspension

Triangle bandages can often be seen in first-aid kits. The triangular bandage suspension is used for bandaging shoulder, clavicle, or upper limb injuries. The procedure is as follows:

1. Have the injured person bend their elbow at a 90-degree angle, with their palms facing inward.

2. Spread a triangular bandage over the injured person, with the two base angles resting on their left and right shoulders, and the vertex angle positioned under their elbow. Wrap the bandage around the forearm.

3. Tie a slip knot with the two base angles and hang the triangular bandage around the injured person's neck.

课文练习 Text Exercises

1. 判断正误。 True or false.

① 我们经常在急救箱中见到三角巾。

② 三角巾有三个角（jiǎo，angle）。

③ 包扎时三角巾的底角放在肘下。

④ 包扎时伤员屈肘 90 度，手掌向上。

2. 选词填空。 Fill in the blanks with the correct words.

| A 活结 | B 锁骨 | C 包裹 | D 急救箱 |

① 我们经常在_____中见到三角巾。

② 三角巾悬吊包扎法适用于肩部外伤、_____外伤或上肢外伤。

③ 用三角巾_____住前臂。

④ 两个底角打_____。

第 24 课 | 三角巾悬吊包扎

学习语法 Grammar

语法点 1　Grammar Point 1

副词：经常　　Adverb: 经常

表示短时间内行为动作发生次数频繁。同"常常"。

It indicates that the action occurs frequently. Same as "常常".

例句：

1. Sānjiǎojīn jīngcháng kěyǐ zài jíjiùxiāng zhōng jiàndào.
三角巾 经常 可以 在 急救箱 中 见到。Triangle bandages can often be seen in first-aid kits.

2. Shǒubù bāozā jīngcháng cǎiyòng bā zì bāozāfǎ.
手部包扎 经常 采用 8 字包扎法。The 8-shape bandaging is often used for hand bandaging.

3. Xībù bāozā jīngcháng cǎiyòng huánxíng bāozāfǎ.
膝部包扎 经常 采用 环形 包扎法。The circular bandaging is often used for knee bandaging.

语法练习 1　Grammar Exercise 1

把"经常"放在句中合适的位置。Put "经常" in the right place in the sentence.

1. 在____急救箱中____可以见到____三角巾。

2. 膝部____包扎____采用什么____包扎法？

3. 急救方法____要____练习（liànxí，practice）____。

4. ____手部外伤____见到____。

231

语法点 2 Grammar Point 2

连词：则 Conjunction: 则

表示前后对比。It indicated the contrast.

例句：
1. 两个底角搭在肩膀上，顶角则放在肘下。Rest the two base angles on the shoulders and the vertex angle under the elbow.
2. 手部包扎用 8 字包扎法，膝部包扎则用环形包扎法。The 8-shape bandaging is used for hand bandaging, while the circular bandaging is used for knee bandaging.
3. 对于重症病人，需要评估所有的身体部位，对于轻症病人，则只需要评估重点部位。For critically ill patients, all body parts need to be assessed. For mild patients, doctors can only assess key parts.

语法练习 2 Grammar Exercise 2

用"则"改写句子。Rewrite the sentences with "则".

1. 没有呼吸、没有心跳，也没有意识的病人，采取仰卧位
   有呼吸、有心跳、没有意识的病人采取侧卧位

2. 重度病情标记为红色 死亡标记为黑色

3. 初级评估能在早期发现威胁生命的状况 次级评估可以获得病人的病史信息

第 24 课 | 三角巾悬吊包扎

4. 测量体温需要 5 分钟　测呼吸需要 30 秒

汉字书写 Writing Chinese Characters

huǒ
火　火 火 火 火
火　火 火 火 火

miè
灭　灭 灭 灭 灭 灭
灭　灭 灭 灭 灭

yán
炎　炎 炎 炎 炎 炎 炎 炎 炎
炎　炎 炎 炎 炎

dēng
灯　灯 灯 灯 灯 灯 灯
灯　灯 灯 灯 灯

职业拓展 Career Insight

Traditional Chinese Medicine Culture

　　Traditional Chinese Medicine contains thousands of years of health and wellness concepts and practical experience of the Chinese nation, and is a great creation of the Chinese nation and a treasure of ancient Chinese science. Traditional Chinese medicine culture includes concepts such as the unity of heaven and man, conforming to the four seasons, balancing form

233

and spirit, and balancing *yin* and *yang*. It is an important component of excellent traditional Chinese culture. Traditional Chinese medicine culture has long been integrated into the daily life of ordinary Chinese people. Some excellent traditional Chinese medicine techniques and products have spread to 196 countries and regions worldwide.

小结 Summary

词语 Words

朗读词语。Read the words aloud.

急救箱	肩	屈肘
包裹	脖子	伤员

语法 Grammar

朗读句子。Read the sentences aloud.

1. 三角巾在急救箱中经常见到。
2. 急救、护理要经常练习。
3. 两个底角搭在肩膀上,顶角则放在肘下。
4. 手部包扎用 8 字包扎法,膝部包扎则用环形包扎法。

第 24 课 | 三角巾悬吊包扎

课文理解 Text Comprehension

根据课文给下列句子排序。**Put the statements in the correct order according to the text.**

1. 把三角巾两个底角搭在伤员的左、右肩上,顶角则放在肘下,包裹住前臂。
2. 把三角巾的两个底角打成一个活结。
3. 伤员屈肘 90 度,掌心向内。
4. 把三角巾悬吊在伤员脖子上。

_____

第25课 Lesson 25

骨折固定 Bone Fixation
Gǔzhé gùdìng

复习 Revision

两人一组，认识三角巾的三个角，并演示用三角巾悬吊包扎前臂。Work in pairs, identify the three angles of a triangle bandage, and demonstrate using a triangle bandage to hang and bind the forearm.

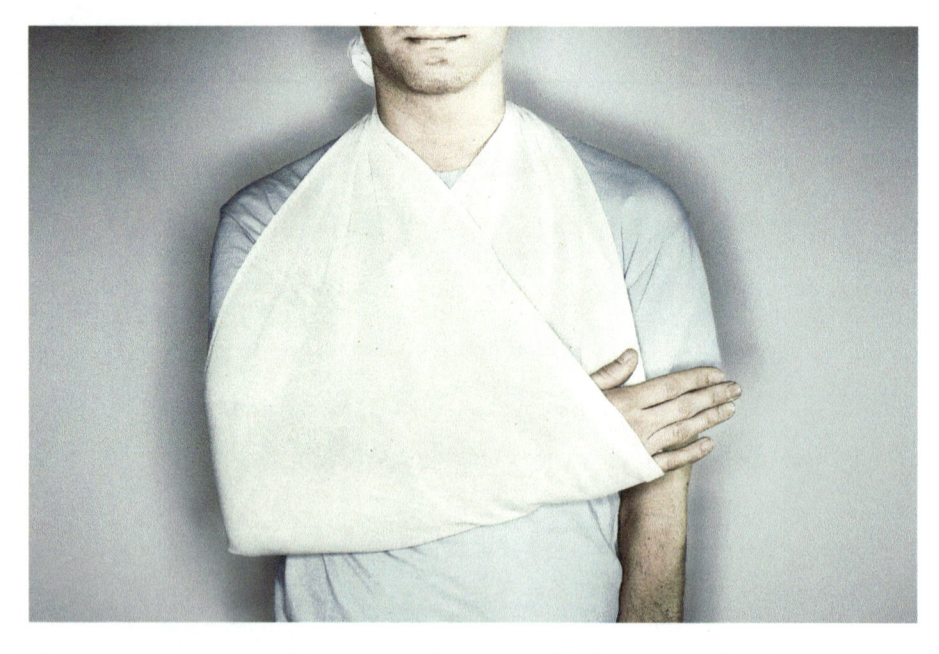

屈肘 —— 铺 —— 搭 —— 放 —— 包裹 —— 打结 —— 悬吊

第 25 课 | 骨折固定

热身 Warming Up

将图片和对应词语连线。 Match the pictures with corresponding words.

1. •   • qīngchuāng 清创 debridement

2. •   • mùbǎn 木板 wooden board

3. •   • shígāo 石膏 gypsum

4. •   • huànyào 换药 change dressing

5. •   • ruǎn 软 soft

6. •   • yìng 硬 hard

237

学习生词 Words and Expressions 25-1

1	技术	jìshù	n.	technique
2	器材	qìcái	n.	equipment
3	多种	duō zhǒng		various
4	材料	cáiliào	n.	material
5	有的	yǒude	pron.	some
6	软	ruǎn	adj.	soft
7	硬	yìng	adj.	hard
8	木板	mùbǎn	n.	wooden board
9	石膏	shígāo	n.	gypsum
10	充气	chōngqì	v.	inflate
11	动作	dòngzuò	n.	movement
12	轻柔	qīngróu	adj.	gentle
13	受伤	shòushāng	v.	injure
14	开放性	kāifàngxìng	n.	open
15	清创	qīngchuāng		debridement
16	换药	huànyào		change dressing

第 25 课 | 骨折固定

词语练习 Words Exercises

1. 看图说词。Look at the pictures and say the words.

2. 朗读短语。Read the phrases aloud.

- 固定器材
- 开放性伤口
- 固定骨折部位
- 给病人清创
- 给病人换药

学习课文 Text 🎧 25-2

Gǔzhé gùdìng
骨折固定

Gùdìng jìshù yòngyú kuàisù gùdìng gǔzhé bùwèi, kěyǐ jiǎnqīng
固定技术用于快速固定骨折部位，可以减轻

239

肿胀和疼痛。固定器材有多种材料。有的材料是软的，例如绷带、三角巾；有的材料是硬的，例如木板、石膏；有的材料是充气的。固定时应该注意：

1. 动作轻柔。
2. 固定范围超过受伤部位上、下关节。
3. 对于开放性伤口，固定前应该清创、换药。

Bone Fixation

Fixation techniques are used to quickly stabilize fractures, which can reduce swelling and pain. There are various materials for fixation equipment. Some materials are soft, such as bandages and triangular bandages; Some materials are hard, such as wooden boards and gypsum; Some materials are inflatable. When performing fixation, the following points should be paid attention to:

1. Handle with gentle movements.
2. Fix beyond the upper and lower joints of the injured area.
3. Perform debridement and dressing changing before fixation for open wounds.

第 25 课 ｜ 骨折固定

课文练习 Text Exercises

1. 判断正误。True or false.

1. 有的固定器材是充气的。
2. 固定时应注意动作轻柔。
3. 固定范围到受伤部位上、下关节。
4. 对于开放性伤口，固定前应清创、换药。

2. 选词填空。Fill in the blanks with the correct words.

| A 清创 | B 技术 | C 轻柔 | D 硬 |

1. 固定_____用于快速固定骨折部位。
2. 固定器材有的是软的，有的是_____的。
3. 固定骨折部位时动作要_____。
4. 对于开放性伤口，固定前应该_____、换药。

学习语法 Grammar

语法点 1 Grammar Point 1

指示代词：有的 Demonstrative pronoun: 有的

指代人或事物中的一部分。
It refers to a part of a group of people or things.

241

例句：
1. 固定器材的材料有的是软的。Some materials for fixation equipment are soft.
2. 有的病人随时有生命危险，要紧急抢救。Some patients are in danger of their lives at any time and require emergency rescue.
3. 有的材料是硬的，例如木板、石膏；有的材料是充气的。Some materials are hard, such as wooden boards and gypsum; Some materials are inflatable.

语法练习 1 Grammar Exercise 1

用"有的"改写句子。Rewrite the sentences with "有的".

1. 固定器材的材料有软的、硬的、充气的。

_____

2. 随时有生命危险的病人，要紧急抢救。

_____

3. 8字包扎法等护理技术需要经常练习。

_____

4. 骨折部位中有一些是开放性伤口，固定前需要清创。

_____

语法点 2 Grammar Point 2

其他结构类型："的"字短语 Other structure category: the 的 phrase

"的"可以附在名词、动词、形容词或短语后，组成"的"字结构，用来指称上下文提到的人或事物，相当于一个名词。

第 25 课 骨折固定

" 的 " can be attached to nouns, verbs, adjectives, or phrases to form the " 的 " phrase, which is used to refer to the person or thing mentioned in the context. It is equivalent to a noun.

例句：
1. 有的材料是软的。Some materials are soft.
   Yǒude cáiliào shì ruǎn de.
2. 木板、石膏等材料是硬的。Materials such as wooden boards and gypsum are hard.
   Mùbǎn, shígāo děng cáiliào shì yìng de.
3. 有的材料是充气的。Some materials are inflatable.
   Yǒude cáiliào shì chōngqì de.

语法练习 2 Grammar Exercise 2

用 " 的 " 字短语改写句子。Rewrite the sentences with the " 的 " phrase.

1. 有的材料是软的材料。

   _____

2. 有的材料是硬的材料。

   _____

3. 有的材料是充气的材料。

   _____

4. 绷带、三角巾等材料是软的材料。

   _____

汉字书写 Writing Chinese Characters

xīn
心 心 心 心
心 心 心 心 心

bì 必 必 必 必 必 必

jí 急 急 急 急 急 急 急 急 急

máng 忙 忙 忙 忙 忙 忙 忙

文化拓展 Culture Insight

The Four Traditional Festivals in China

The Spring Festival, Qingming Festival, Dragon Boat Festival and Mid-Autumn Festival are four important traditional festivals in China. These festivals have a long history, deep cultural significance, and are celebrated with rich folk activities.

The Spring Festival is the most important traditional festival in China and marks the beginning of the Chinese new year. It falls on the first to the fifteenth day of the first lunar month. The theme of the Spring Festival is to bid farewell to the old year and welcome the new one, and it is celebrated with a wide range of folk activities. The history of the Spring Festival dates back to more than two thousand years ago.

Qingming is one of the twenty-four solar terms in the Chinese calendar. It is a traditional festival for ancestor worship, typically observed between April 4th and 6th in the Chinese calendar. The theme of Qingming is to honor and mourn the passing of loved ones. It is also a time for spring outings.

The Dragon Boat Festival falls on the fifth day of the fifth lunar month. It is celebrated with various activities related to dragons, such as dragon boat races, hanging mugwort leaves, drinking realgar wine, and wearing protective charms to ward off evil spirits and disease.

The Mid-Autumn Festival is on the 15th day of the eighth month of the lunar calendar. It's a great time for family reunion and enjoying the beauty of full moon together.

小结 Summary

词语 Words

朗读词语。Read the words aloud.

受伤	器材	石膏
开放性伤口	清创	换药

语法 Grammar

朗读句子。Read the sentences aloud.

1. 有的材料是软的，例如绷带、三角巾。
2. 有的材料是硬的，例如木板、石膏。

课文理解 Text Comprehension

根据课文内容回答问题。Answer the questions according to the text.

1. 为什么要固定骨折部位?

   _____

2. 硬的固定材料有什么?软的有什么?

   _____

3. 骨折固定的范围是什么?

   _____

4. 对于有开放性伤口的骨折,固定前需要做什么?

   _____

第26课 Lesson 26

Qiánbì gǔzhé chǔlǐ
前臂骨折处理
Forearm Fixation

复习 Revision

填写正确的答案。Fill in the blanks with the correct answers.

固定骨折部位时应该注意：

1. 动作_____。
2. 固定范围超过受伤部位_____。
3. 对于开放性伤口，固定前应该_____、_____。

热身 Warming Up

看图选词。Look at the pictures and choose the correct words.

A 夹板 (jiābǎn) splint　　B 人文关怀 (rénwén guānhuái) humanistic care
C 流程 (liúchéng) process　　D 坐位 (zuòwèi) sitting position

247

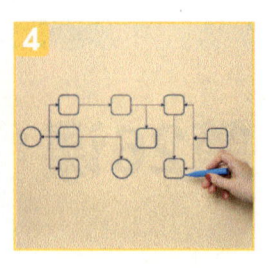

学习生词 Words and Expressions 🎧 26-1

1	流程	liúchéng	*n.*	process
2	伤情	shāngqíng	*n.*	injury
3	协助	xiézhù	*v.*	assist
4	坐位	zuòwèi	*n.*	sitting position
5	挑选	tiāoxuǎn	*v.*	select
6	块	kuài	*measure word*	piece
7	合适	héshì	*adj.*	suitable
8	夹板	jiābǎn	*n.*	splint
9	放	fàng	*v.*	place
10	伤肢	shāngzhī	*n.*	injured limb

11	起来	qǐlái	v.	rise up
12	指端	zhǐduān	n.	fingertip
13	询问	xúnwèn	v.	inquire
14	感受	gǎnshòu	v.	feel
15	人文关怀	rénwén guānhuái		humanistic care
16	周	zhōu	n.	week

词语练习 Words Exercises

1. 看图说词。Look at the pictures and say the words.

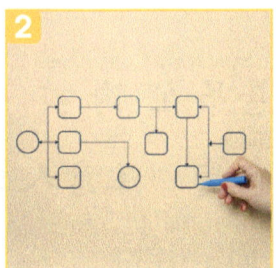

2. 朗读词语搭配。Read the collocations aloud.

评估伤情　　　　人文关怀

采取坐位　　　　询问感受

学习课文 Text 🎧 26-2

前臂骨折处理

前臂骨折包扎固定技术的操作流程如下：

1. 评估病人伤情。
2. 协助病人采取坐位。前臂屈肘90度。
3. 挑选一块合适的夹板放在伤肢下。
4. 用绷带把伤肢和夹板包扎起来。露出指端。
5. 用三角巾把伤肢悬吊在胸前。
6. 询问病人的疼痛感受。注意人文关怀。
7. 固定时间是4—8周。

Forearm Fixation

The procedure for bandaging and fixation of a forearm fracture is as follows:

1. Assess the patient's injury condition.

2. Assist the patient in taking a sitting position and bend the forearm to a 90-degree angle.

3. Select a suitable splint and place it under the injured limb.

4. Wrap the injured limb and splint with bandages, leaving the fingertips exposed.

5. Suspend the injured limb in front of the chest with a triangular bandage.

6. Inquire about the patient's pain level. Ensure humanistic care.

7. The time for fixation is 4–8 weeks.

课文练习 Text Exercises

1. 判断正误。True or false.

1. 前臂骨折包扎固定时病人采取坐位。
2. 前臂骨折包扎固定时不要用木板。
3. 急救护理时要注意人文关怀。
4. 前臂骨折的固定时间是4—8周。

2. 根据课文内容回答问题。Answer the questions according to the text.

1. 前臂骨折包扎前要先做什么？

_____

2. 病人前臂屈肘多少度？

_____

3 前臂骨折包扎使用什么材料？

_____

4 为什么要询问病人的疼痛感受？

_____

学习语法 Grammar

语法点 1　Grammar Point 1

特殊句型：连动句2　Special sentence pattern: the sentence with a serial verb construction 2

两个谓语动词共用一个主语时，两个动词短语可以表示先后的连续动作。
When two predicate verbs share the same subject, the two verb phrases can indicate the actions happen successively.

例句：

1 挑选一块合适的夹板 放在 伤肢 下。
Tiāoxuǎn yí kuài héshì de jiābǎn fàng zài shāngzhī xià.
Select a suitable splint and place it under the injured limb.

2 摆好病人的体位进行 抢救。
Bǎihǎo bìngrén de tǐwèi jìnxíng qiǎngjiù.
Position the patient properly and proceed with rescue.

3 护士 甩好温度计测量 病人的体温。
Hùshi shuǎihǎo wēndùjì cèliáng bìngrén de tǐwēn.
The nurse swung the thermometer to measure the patient's body temperature.

第 26 课 | 前臂骨折处理

语法练习 1　Grammar Exercise 1

按照正确的语序连词成句。Make sentences in correct orders with the given words or phrases.

1　①挑选　②一块合适的夹板　③护士　④放在　⑤伤肢下

_____

2　①医生　②摆好　③进行抢救　④病人的体位

_____

3　①病人　②休息　③坐下来

_____

4　①护士　②给病人　③测体温　④甩好温度计

_____

语法点 2　Grammar Point 2

补语：趋向补语 2　The complement: the complement of direction 2

"上来、下去、出来、进去、起来、过来"这样的复合趋向动词，可以放在动词的后面，补充说明动作的方向。

Compound directional verbs such as "上来，下去，出来，进去，起来，过来" can be used after a verb to supplement the direction of the action.

例句：

1　用绷带把伤肢和夹板包扎起来。Wrap the injured limb and splint with bandages.
　　Yòng bēngdài bǎ shāngzhī hé jiābǎn bāozā qǐlái.

2　医生让病人把胳膊伸出来。The doctor asked the patient to extend his arm.
　　Yīshēng ràng bìngrén bǎ gēbo shēn chūlái.

3　病人的体温降（decrease）下去了。The patient's body temperature has decreased.
　　Bìngrén de tǐwēn jiàng xiàqù le.

253

语法练习 2 Grammar Exercise 2

选词填空。Fill in the blanks with the correct words.

> A 起来　　　　　　　　B 出来

1. 用绷带把伤肢和夹板包扎＿＿＿＿＿。
2. 包扎时，病人的指端要露＿＿＿＿＿。
3. 前臂要用三角巾在脖子处悬挂＿＿＿＿＿。
4. 手术结束，医生从手术室里走＿＿＿＿＿。

汉字书写 Writing Chinese Characters

bā
巴　巴 巴 巴 巴

sè
色　色 色 色 色 色

bǎ
把　把 把 把 把 把

bà
爸　爸 爸 爸 爸 爸

职业拓展 Career Insight

Humanistic Care in Nursing

Humanistic care in nursing refers to the delivery of personalized and compassionate care by nursing staff during medical treatment, focusing on both the physical and psychological needs of patients. The goal is to promote recovery and enhance the quality of life. Common humanistic care measures in nursing include: emotional support, effective communication, health education, pain management, nutritional support, a comfortable environment, and education guidance.

小结 Summary

词语 Words

朗读词语。Read the words aloud.

伤情	坐位	夹板
伤肢	感受	人文关怀

语法 Grammar

朗读句子。Read the sentences aloud.

1. 挑选一块合适的夹板放在伤肢下。

② 摆好体位进行抢救。

③ 用绷带把伤肢和夹板包扎起来。

④ 用三角巾把伤肢悬吊起来。

课文理解 Text Comprehension

根据课文内容给下列句子排序。Put the statements in the correct order according to the text.

① 挑选一块合适的夹板放于伤肢下面。

② 用绷带把伤肢和夹板包扎起来。露出指端。

③ 评估病人伤情。

④ 协助病人采取坐位。前臂屈肘 90°。

⑤ 用三角巾将伤肢悬吊于胸前。

第27课 Lesson 27

Xiǎotuǐ gǔzhé chǔlǐ
小腿骨折处理
Lower Leg Fixation

复习 Revision

朗读短语。Read the phrases aloud.

- 固定技术
- 操作流程
- 采取坐位
- 询问病人
- 疼痛的感受
- 人文关怀

热身 Warming Up

看图选词。Look at the pictures and choose the correct words.

A 足跟 (zúgēn) heel
B 脚趾 (jiǎozhǐ) toe
C 小腿 (xiǎotuǐ) lower leg
D 腓骨 (féigǔ) fibula

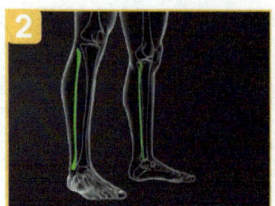

学习生词 Words and Expressions 27-1

1	小腿	xiǎotuǐ	*n.*	lower leg
2	胫骨	jìnggǔ	*n.*	tibia
3	腓骨	féigǔ	*n.*	fibula
4	条	tiáo	*measure word*	(used for sth. long, narrow or thin)
5	分别	fēnbié	*adv.*	respectively
6	内侧	nèicè	*n.*	inner side
7	外侧	wàicè	*n.*	outer side
8	隆突	lóngtū		protrusion
9	长度	chángdù	*n.*	length

10	相当	xiāngdāng	v.	be equivalent to
11	足（脚）跟	zú (jiǎo) gēn	n.	heel
12	并且	bìngqiě	conj.	and
13	端	duān	n.	end
14	脚趾	jiǎozhǐ	n.	toe
15	过紧	guò jǐn		overtight
16	重新	chóngxīn	adv.	afresh

词语练习 Words Exercises

1. 看图说词。Look at the pictures and say the words.

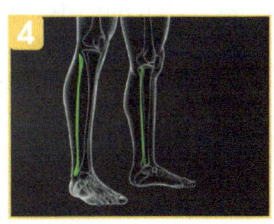

2. 两人一组，指出下列人体部位。Work in pairs, and point out the following human body parts.

1. 腿：大腿　　小腿　　胫骨　　腓骨
2. 脚：足（脚）跟　　脚趾

学习课文 Text 🎧 27-2

小腿骨折处理

小腿骨折包括胫骨骨折和腓骨骨折。固定流程如下：

1. 护士协助伤员采取仰卧位。
2. 在伤员腿下放三条绷带。
3. 把夹板分别放在伤肢的内侧和外侧，在骨隆突处加棉垫。两块夹板的长度相当于从足跟到膝部的长度。
4. 用绷带固定夹板，并且在骨折部位的两端打结。
5. 如果脚趾青紫，可能是包扎过紧，应该重新固定。

Lower Leg Fixation

Lower leg fractures include fractures of the tibia and fibula.

The procedure for fixation is as follows:

1. The nurse assists the injured person in lying flat.

2. Place three bandages under the injured leg.

3. Position the splints on the inner and outer sides of the injured limb, adding cotton pads over the bony protrusions. The length of the two splints is equivalent to that from the heel to the knee.

4. Fix the splint with bandages and tie knots at both ends of the fracture.

5. If the toes turn blue or purple, it may indicate overtight wrapping, and the fixation should be re-fixed.

课文练习 Text Exercises

1. 判断正误。True or false.

1 小腿骨折时，护士协助伤员采取坐位。

2 小腿骨折时，护士把夹板分别放在伤肢的内侧和外侧。

3 小腿骨折时，两块夹板的长度相当于从足跟到膝部的长度。

4 如果脚趾青紫，可能是包扎过紧，应重新固定。

2. 选词填空。Fill in the blanks with the correct words.

1 小腿骨折包括胫骨和_____骨折。

　　A 足跟　　　　B 腓骨　　　　C 脚趾

2 护士协助伤员采取_____位。

　　A 仰卧　　　　B 侧卧　　　　C 坐

3 在腿下放置三_____绷带。

　A 个　　　　　B 名　　　　　C 条

4 将夹板分别放在伤肢的内侧和_____。

　A 旁边　　　　B 外侧　　　　C 中间

学习语法 Grammar

语法点 1　Grammar Point 1

量词小结　Summary of measure words

汉语的量词有名量词和动量词两种。"个、种、条、分钟"等都是名量词,"次、针"等是动量词。名量词放在所修饰的名词前,动量词放在所补充说明的动词后。

Chinese measure words include the quantifiers for nouns and the quantifiers for verbs. The measure words such as "个,种,条,分钟" are quantifiers for nouns, while the measure words like "次,针" are quantifiers for verbs. The quantifiers for nouns are used before the noun, and the quantifiers for verbs are used after the verb.

例句：

1　Zài tuǐ xià fàng sān tiáo bēngdài.
在腿下放 三条 绷带。Place three bandages under the leg.

2　Liǎng kuài jiābǎn de chángdù xiāngdāngyú cóng zúgēn dào xībù de chángdù.
两块夹板的长度相当于从足跟到膝部的长度。
The length of the two splints is equivalent to that from the heel to the knee.

3　Zhèzhǒng yào měi tiān chī liǎng cì.
这种 药每天吃 两次。The medication should be taken twice a day.

语法练习 1 Grammar Exercise 1

选词填空。Fill in the blanks with the correct words.

    A 个   B 种   C 条   D 块

1. 在腿下放三_____绷带。
2. 两_____夹板的长度相当于从足跟到膝部的长度。
3. 在骨折两端打一_____结。
4. 固定器材有多_____材料。

语法点 2 Grammar Point 2

连词：并且 Conjunction: 并且

"并且"连接两个分句，放在第二个句子的开头，表示更进一层。

"并且" connects two clauses and is used at the beginning of the second clause, indicating going further.

例句：

1. Yòng bēngdài gùdìng jiābǎn, bìngqiě zài gǔzhé bùwèi de liǎng duān dǎjié.
用 绷带 固定 夹板，并且 在 骨折 部位 的 两 端 打结。Fix the splint with bandages and tie knots at both ends of the fracture.

2. Bāozā gùdìng gǔzhé de qiánbì, bìngqiě xúnwèn bìngrén de téngtòng gǎnshòu.
包扎 固定 骨折 的 前臂，并且 询问 病人 的 疼痛 感受。Wrap and fix the fractured forearm, and inquire about the patient's pain level.

3. Ràng bìngrén zuòxià, bìngqiě qiánbì qūzhǒu jiǔshí dù.
让 病人 坐下，并且 前臂 屈肘 90 度。Have the patient sit down and bend their forearm to a 90-degree angle.

语法练习 2　Grammar Exercise 2

用"并且"完成句子。Complete the sentences with "并且".

1. 用绷带固定夹板　　在腿下放三条绷带

_____

2. 用绷带固定夹板　　在骨折部位的两端打结

_____

3. 用三角巾固定好上肢　　询问病人的疼痛感受

_____

4. 骨折固定时要选择合适的固定材料　　动作要轻柔

_____

汉字书写　Writing Chinese Characters

dōng
东　东 东 东 东 东

xī
西　西 西 西 西 西

nán
南　南 南 南 南 南 南 南 南

běi
北　北 北 北 北

文化拓展 Culture Insight

China's High-speed Railway

The total operating mileage of China's high-speed rail network has reached 42,000 kilometers, firmly ranking first in the world. China's high-speed railway is the fastest-growing, most technologically advanced, and has the strongest integration capabilities, the longest operating mileage, the highest operating speed, and the largest scale of high-speed rail construction projects worldwide.

In terms of operating speed, the maximum design speed of the trains can reach 350 kilometers per hour. Regarding transportation capacity, a long train set can carry over 1,000 passengers and depart every 3 minutes, offering substantial transportation capacity. In terms of adapting to the natural environment, high-speed trains can operate around the clock, largely unaffected by rain, snow, or fog. In terms of energy conservation and environmental protection, high-speed rail is an environmentally friendly mode of transportation that meets the requirements for energy efficiency and emission reduction.

小结 Summary

词语 Words

朗读词语。Read the words aloud.

胫骨	腓骨	仰卧位
隆突	足跟	脚趾

语法 Grammar

朗读句子。Read the sentences aloud.

1. 在伤员腿下放三条绷带。
2. 两块夹板的长度相当于从足跟到膝部的长度。
3. 用绷带固定夹板,并且在骨折部位的两端打结。
4. 让伤员采取仰卧位,并且在伤员腿下放三条绷带。

课文理解 Text Comprehension

根据课文内容给下列句子排序。Put the statements in the correct order according to the text.

1. 把夹板分别放在伤肢的内侧和外侧。
2. 在腿下面放置三条绷带。
3. 护士协助伤员采取仰卧位。
4. 用绷带固定夹板,并且在骨折部位的两端打结。

第28课 Lesson 28

Bānyùn shāngyuán
搬运伤员
Handling the Injured

复习 Revision

根据课文内容回答问题。Answer the questions according to the text.

1. 小腿骨折包括哪（nǎ，which）两种？

   _____

2. 护士协助伤员采取坐位还是仰卧位？

   _____

3. 放在伤肢两侧的夹板有多长？

   _____

4. 脚趾青紫，可能是什么造成（zàochéng，cause）的？应该马上做什么？

   _____

急救护理（基里巴斯版） 初级篇

热身 Warming Up

将图片和对应的词语连线。Match the pictures with the corresponding words.

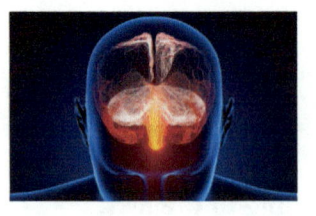

1 • • bānyùn 搬运 handle

2 • • shénjīng 神经 nerve

3 • • dānjià 担架 stretcher

4 • • fǔwò 俯卧 take a prone position

学习生词 Words and Expressions 🎧 28-1

1	搬运	bānyùn	v.	handle
2	转运	zhuǎnyùn	v.	transport
3	活动	huódòng	v.	move

268

第 28 课 ｜ 搬运伤员

4	受限	shòuxiàn		restricted
5	根据	gēnjù	prep.	according to
6	选择	xuǎnzé	v.	choose
7	当	dāng	prep.	when
8	神经	shénjīng	n.	nerve
9	禁止	jìnjì	v.	prohibit
10	俯卧	fǔwò	v.	take a prone position
11	担架	dānjià	n.	stretcher
12	平稳	píngwěn	adj.	stable

词语练习 Words Exercises

1. 看图说词。 Look at the pictures and say the words.

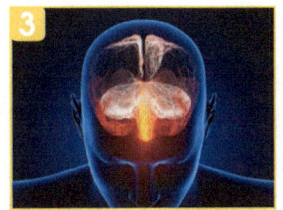

2. 朗读词语搭配。 Read the collocations aloud.

搬运病人　　转运病人　　禁止搬运　　平稳搬运

根据情况　　情况紧急　　损伤神经　　损伤血管

侧卧——仰卧——俯卧

269

学习课文 Text 🎧 28-2

搬运 伤员
Bānyùn shāngyuán

搬运技术用于转运活动受限的病人。应该根据情况选择适宜的方法。当情况不紧急时，先包扎伤口再搬运病人。如果搬运会损伤神经和血管，禁止搬运。如果病人昏迷，就让病人侧卧或俯卧在担架上。注意搬运时要平稳。

Handling the Injured

Transportation techniques are used to move patients with limited mobility. The appropriate method should be chosen according to the situation. When the situation is not urgent, first bandage the wound before moving the patient. If the handling may pose a risk of damaging nerves or blood vessels, handling is prohibited. If the patient is unconscious, place them on their side or prone on a stretcher. Ensure that the patient is handled steadily and carefully.

课文练习 Text Exercises

1. 判断正误。True or false.
   1. 搬运技术用于转运不能自己活动的伤员。
   2. 当情况紧急时，可以先包扎伤口再搬运病人。
   3. 如果搬运会损伤神经和血管，就不能搬运。
   4. 搬运时要平稳。

2. 选词填空。Fill in the blanks with the correct words.
   1. 搬运技术用于转运_____受限的伤员。
      A 活动　　　　B 上臂　　　　C 肘部
   2. 应根据情况_____适宜的方法。
      A 转运　　　　B 搬运　　　　C 选择
   3. 如果搬运会损伤_____和血管，禁止搬运。
      A 头　　　　　B 小腿　　　　C 神经
   4. 如果病人昏迷，就让病人_____或俯卧在担架上。
      A 侧卧　　　　B 仰卧　　　　C 坐

学习语法 Grammar

语法点 1 Grammar Point 1

介词：根据　Preposition: 根据

"根据"引介动作行为的前提或依据的事物，组成的介词结构可以放在句首。
The prepositional structure formed by the preposition "根据" introducing the premise or basis of the behavior can be placed at the beginning of a sentence.

例句：

1. <small>Yīnggāi gēnjù bìngrén de qíngkuàng xuǎnzé shìyí de bānyùn fāngfǎ.</small>
应该根据病人的情况选择适宜的搬运方法。The appropriate handling method should be chosen based on the patient's condition.

2. <small>Gēnjù zhège bìngrén de qíngkuàng, kěyǐ xiān bāozā shāngkǒu zài bānyùn.</small>
根据这个病人的情况，可以先包扎伤口再搬运。Based on the patient's condition, the wound can be bandaged before transportation.

3. <small>Gēnjù bìngrén de hūxī zhuàngkuàng, yīnggāi shǐyòng qìguǎn chāguǎn.</small>
根据病人的呼吸状况，应该使用气管插管。According to the patient's respiratory condition, tracheal intubation should be used.

语法练习 1 Grammar Exercise 1

用"根据"完成句子。Complete the sentences with "根据".

1. 病人的情况　　选择适宜的搬运方法

_____

2. 病人的呼吸状况　　应该使用气管插管

_____

3. 这个病人的情况　　可以先包扎伤口再搬运

_____

4. 病人的脚趾青紫程度　　需要重新固定绷带

_____

语法点 2 Grammar Point 2

假设复句：如果……就…… Supportive complex sentence: with correlatives "如果 ... 就 ..."

"如果……就……"连接假设复句，第一个分句提出假设，第二个分句是这一假设条件下的推论或结果。

"如果 ... 就 ..." connects supportive complex sentences, where the first clause proposes the hypothesis, and the second clause is the inference or result under this hypothetical condition.

例句：

1. 如果病人昏迷，就让病人侧卧或俯卧在担架上。If the patient is unconscious, place them on their side or prone on a stretcher.

2. 如果情况不紧急，就先包扎伤口再搬运病人。If the situation is not urgent, first bandage the wound before moving the patient.

3. 如果搬运会损伤神经和血管，就不能搬运病人。If the handling may pose a risk of damaging nerves or blood vessels, the patient cannot be transported.

语法练习 2 Grammar Exercise 2

用"如果……就……"完成句子。Complete the sentences with "如果 ... 就 ...".

1. 病人昏迷　　让病人侧卧在担架上

2. 包扎过紧　　重新包扎

3. 情况不紧急　　先包扎伤口再搬运病人

4 搬运会损伤神经和血管　　不要搬运病人

汉字书写 Writing Chinese Characters

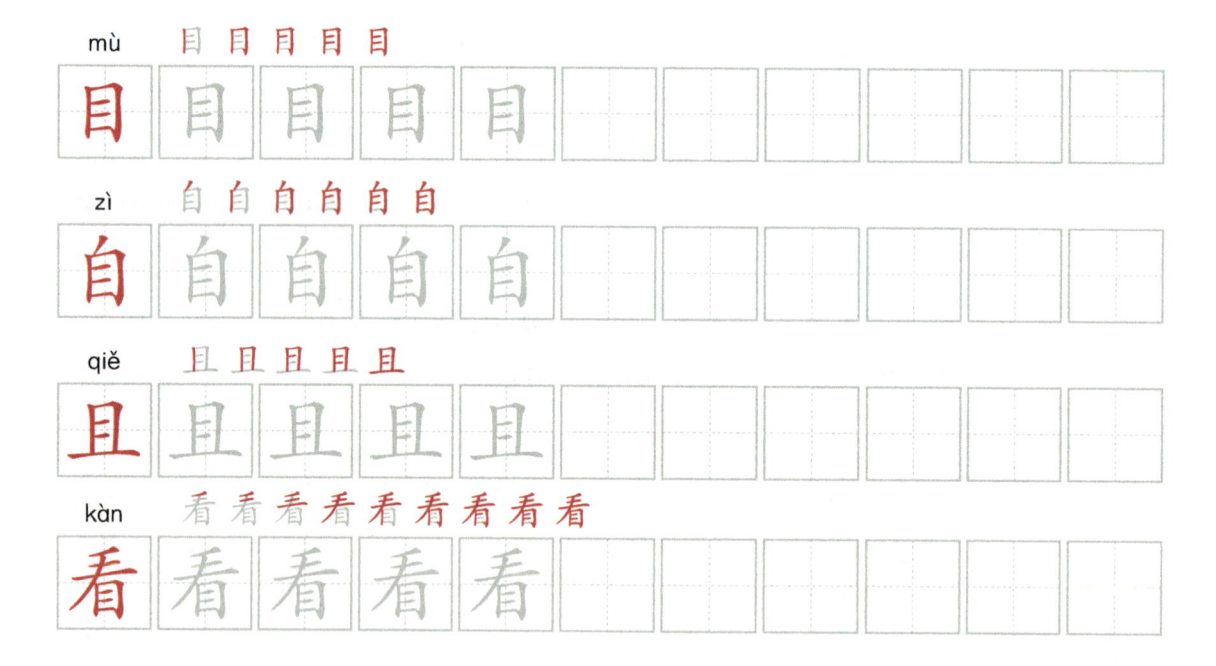

mù
目　目 目 目 目 目

zì
自　自 自 自 自 自

qiě
且　且 且 且 且 且

kàn
看　看 看 看 看 看 看 看 看 看

职业拓展 Career Insight

Palliative Care

Palliative care, also known as end-of-life care, focuses on providing relief to patients with serious, life-limiting illnesses. In 2017, the National Health and Family Planning Commission of China issued the "Guidelines for Palliative Care Practice (Trial)", which formally introduced the term

"Palliative Care". It refers to a multidisciplinary, patient-and-family-centered approach that aims to provide comprehensive care, including physical, psychological, and spiritual support. The goal of palliative care is to manage symptoms, alleviate pain and discomfort, improve the quality of life, and help patients pass away comfortably, peacefully, and with dignity. Ultimately, it strives to achieve a peaceful death, a dignified life, and a peaceful environment for both the patients and their families.

小结 Summary

词语 Words

朗读词语。Read the words aloud.

| 搬运 | 转运 | 担架 |
| 神经 | 侧卧 | 俯卧 |

语法 Grammar

朗读句子。Read the sentences aloud.

1. 如果情况不紧急，就先包扎伤口再搬运病人。
2. 如果病人昏迷，就让病人侧卧或俯卧在担架上。
3. 根据情况选择适宜的方法。
4. 根据病人的脚趾青紫程度，重新固定绷带。

课文理解 Text Comprehension

根据课文内容选词填空。Fill in the blanks with correct words according to the text.

> A 平稳　　　　　B 根据情况　　　　C 包扎伤口
> D 活动受限　　　E 神经和血管　　　F 侧卧或俯卧

1. 搬运技术用于转运_____的病人。
2. 应该_____选择适宜的方法。
3. 当情况不紧急时，先_____再搬运病人。
4. 如果搬运会损伤_____，禁止搬运。
5. 如果病人昏迷，就让病人_____在担架上。
6. 搬运时注意要_____。

第29课 Lesson 29

双人搬运
Shuāng rén bānyùn
Two-man Handling

复习 Revision

根据课文内容回答问题。Answer the questions according to the text.

1. 什么病人需要搬运？
   _____

2. 应该根据什么选择搬运的方法？
   _____

3. 如果搬运会损伤神经和血管，可以搬运吗？
   _____

4. 如果病人昏迷，让病人侧卧还是俯卧在担架上？
   _____

热身 Warming Up

看图选词。Look at the pictures and choose the correct words.

A 椅子 yǐzi chair　　B 双人 shuāng rén two people
C 握 wò hold　　D 背 bèi back

1 　2 　3 　4

学习生词 Words and Expressions 🎧 29-1

1	双人	shuāng rén		two people
2	还是	háishi	*conj.*	or
3	一般情况下	yìbān qíngkuàng xià		generally
4	伤势	shāngshì	*n.*	injury
5	较	jiào	*adv.*	rather
6	重	zhòng	*adj.*	severe

第 29 课 | 双人搬运

7	轻	qīng	*adj.*	mild
8	人员	rényuán	*n.*	staff
9	紧	jǐn	*adj.*	tight
10	地	de	*aux.*	(used with an adverb or adverbial phrase)
11	握	wò	*v.*	hold
12	一起	yìqǐ	*adv.*	together
13	把	bǎ	*measure word*	(used for somthing with a handle)
14	椅子	yǐzi	*n.*	chair
15	只	zhī	*measure word*	(used for one of certain paired things)
16	背	bèi	*n.*	back
17	靠	kào	*v.*	lean against
18	另	lìng	*pron.*	another

词语练习 Words Exercises

1. 看图说词。 Look at the pictures and say the words.

279

2. 朗读短语。Read the phrases aloud.

双人搬运	多人搬运	担架搬运
伤势较重	伤势较轻	一把椅子
一只手臂	另一只手臂	一般情况下

学习课文 Text 29-2

双人搬运
Shuāng rén bānyùn

转运病人时，是双人搬运、多人搬运还是担架搬运？一般情况下，担架搬运适用于伤势较重的病人；多人搬运适用于脊柱损伤的病人；双人搬运适用于伤势较轻的病人。

双人搬运的方法是：两个搬运人员的手紧紧地握在一起，像一把椅子。伤员坐在搬运人员的一只手臂上，背靠另一只手臂。

第 29 课　双人搬运

Two-man Handling

When transporting patients, are they transported by two people, multiple people, or stretchers? Generally, stretcher handling is suitable for patients with severe injuries; Multi-person handling is suitable for patients with spinal injuries; Two-man handling is suitable for patients with milder conditions.

The method of two-man handling is to hold the hands of two people tightly together, like a chair. The injured person sits on one set of arms, leaning back against the other.

课文练习　Text Exercises

1. 判断正误。True or false.

① 担架搬运适用于伤势较重的病人。

② 双人搬运适用于病情较重的病人。

③ 多人搬运适用于脊柱损伤的病人。

④ 双人搬运时，两人的手紧紧地握在担架上。

2. 选词填空。Fill in the blanks with the correct words.

① 一般情况下，担架搬运适用于伤势较_____的病人。

　A 高　　　　　B 重　　　　　C 轻

2 多人搬运适用于_____损伤的病人。

　　A 脊柱　　　　B 上臂　　　　C 肘部

3 双人搬运适用于病情较_____的病人。

　　A 高　　　　　B 重　　　　　C 轻

4 两名搬运人员的手紧紧地握在一起，像一把_____。

　　A 椅子　　　　B 担架　　　　C 俯卧

学习语法 Grammar

语法点 1　Grammar Point 1

提问的方法：用"还是"提问　Way of asking questions: questions with "还是"

连词"还是"表示选择关系，多用于疑问句，要求答话人选择其一回答。

The conjunction "还是" indicates an alternative relation, often used in interrogative sentences, requiring the respondent to choose one answer.

例句：

1 Shì shuāng rén bānyùn, duō rén bānyùn háishi dānjià bānyùn?
是双人搬运、多人搬运还是担架搬运？ Is it two-man handling, multi-person handling, or stretcher handling?

2 Yòng zhǐyāfǎ háishi jiāyā bāozāfǎ gěi bìngrén zhǐxiě?
用指压法还是加压包扎法给病人止血？ Do you use finger-pressing manipulation or pressure bandaging to stop bleeding for patients?

3 Xuándiào bāozā shǐyòng bēngdài háishi sānjiǎojīn?
悬吊包扎使用绷带还是三角巾？ Do you use bandages or triangular bandages for suspension dressing?

第 29 课 | 双人搬运

语法练习 1 Grammar Exercise 1

用"还是"改写下列句子。Rewrite the sentences with " 还是 ".

1. 转运病人，使用_____?（双人搬运 / 多人搬运）
2. 悬吊包扎使用_____?（绷带 / 三角巾）
3. 用_____给病人止血?（指压法 / 加压法）
4. 踝部外伤包扎用_____?（8 字包扎法 / 环形包扎法）

语法点 2 Grammar Point 2

单音节形容词重叠：AA Reduplication of monosyllabic adjectives: AA

汉语中有一部分形容词可以重叠，重叠后表示性质、状态的程度加深。单音节形容词按 AA 式重叠。口语中，有些形容词重叠后第二个音节变为第一声并儿化。形容词重叠后作状语时常加"地"。

There are some adjectives which can be reduplicated to express the deepening of its nature, state or degree. Monosyllabic adjectives are reduplicated as the form of AA. In oral language, the second syllable of some words will be pronounced as the first tone and rhotic after reduplication. The reduplication of adjectives are often followed by "地" when serving as adverbials.

例句：
1. 两个搬运人员的手紧紧地握在一起。The hands of the two people were tightly held together.
   Liǎng gè bānyùn rényuán de shǒu jǐnjǐn de wò zài yìqǐ.
2. 搬运病人时要慢慢（slowly）地搬运。The patient needs to be transported slowly.
   Bānyùn bìngrén shí yào mànmàn de bānyùn.
3. 医生和护士把病人轻轻地放在担架上。Doctors and nurses gently put the patient on a stretcher.
   Yīshēng hé hùshi bǎ bìngrén qīngqīng de fàng zài dānjià shàng.

语法练习 2 Grammar Exercise 2

按照正确的语序连词成句。Make sentences in correct orders with the given words or phrases.

1. ①两个搬运人员 ②的 ③握在一起 ④手 ⑤紧紧地

2. ①把 ②要 ③病人 ④放在 ⑤轻轻地 ⑥担架上

3. ①让 ②慢慢地 ③病人 ④侧卧 ⑤在担架上

4. ①病人 ②椅子 ③握住 ④紧紧地

汉字书写 Writing Chinese Characters

tóu 头 头 头 头 头 头

jiá 夹 夹 夹 夹 夹 夹

mǎi 买 买 买 买 买 买

第 29 课 | 双人搬运

mài
卖 卖 卖 卖 卖 卖 卖 卖 卖

文化拓展 Culture Insight

WeChat

WeChat is a free application launched by Tencent on January 21, 2011, that provides instant messaging services for smart devices. WeChat supports communication across different operators and operating system platforms, allowing users to quickly send free voice messages, videos, images, and text messages (requiring only a small amount of network daga). In addition, WeChat offers various service plugins such as "Shake", "Moments", "Public Platform", and "Voice Notepad" which enable users to share streaming content and use location-based social features. This app also includes functions like public platform, social media, and message push notifications. Users can share content with friends or post exciting content they encounter on WeChat's social media features.

As of 2023, WeChat has over 1.3 billion users.

小结 Summary

词语 Words

填写正确的答案。Fill in the blanks with the correct answers.

1. 搬运：_____搬运　　　_____搬运　　　_____搬运
2. 伤势：伤势_____　　　伤势_____
   一_____椅子　　　一_____手臂

语法 Grammar

朗读句子。Read the sentences aloud.

1. 转运病人时，是双人搬运、多人搬运还是担架搬运？
2. 多人搬运是三人搬运、四人搬运还是五人搬运？
3. 两个搬运人员的手紧紧地握在一起。
4. 病人紧紧地握住椅子。

课文理解 Text Comprehension

根据课文内容选词填空。Fill in the blanks with the correct words according to the text.

A 背靠　　B 紧紧地　　C 一只手臂　　D 一把椅子　　E 病情较轻

　　双人搬运适用于_____的病人。两个搬运人员的手_____握在一起，像_____。伤员坐在搬运人员的_____上，_____另一只手臂。

第30课 Lesson 30

多人搬运
Duō rén bānyùn
Multi-people Handling

复习 Revision

根据课文内容回答问题。Answer the questions according to the text.

1. 转运病人时，根据什么选择双人搬运、多人搬运或担架搬运？

   _____

2. 担架搬运适用于什么病人？

   _____

3. 多人搬运适用于什么病人？

   _____

4. 双人搬运适用于什么病人？

   _____

热身 Warming Up

将图片和对应词语连线。Match the pictures with corresponding words.

1 •   • jǐngzhuī 颈椎 cervical vertebra

2 •   • yāozhuī 腰椎 lumbar vertebra

3 •   • túnbù 臀部 buttocks

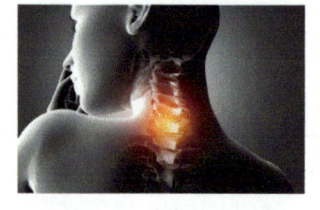

4 •   • dūn 蹲 squat

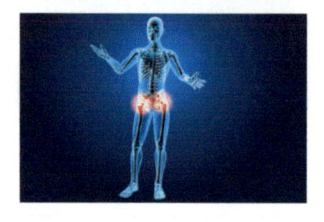

学习生词 Words and Expressions 🎧 30-1

| 1 | 一定 | yídìng | *adv.* | must |
| 2 | 保持 | bǎochí | *v.* | keep |

第 30 课 | 多人搬运

3	伸直	shēnzhí	v.	(keep) straight
4	颈椎	jǐngzhuī	n.	cervical vertebra
5	者	zhě	suffix	(used after a noun phrase to indicate a person in the state)
6	蹲	dūn	v.	squat
7	同侧	tóng cè		same side
8	托	tuō	v.	support
9	臀部	túnbù	n.	buttocks
10	下肢	xiàzhī	n.	lower limbs
11	喊	hǎn	v.	shout
12	口令	kǒulìng	n.	words of command
13	硬质	yìng zhì		hard
14	腰椎	yāozhuī	n.	lumbar vertebra
15	但	dàn	conj.	but

词语练习 Words Exercises

1. 看图说词。 Look at the pictures and say the words.

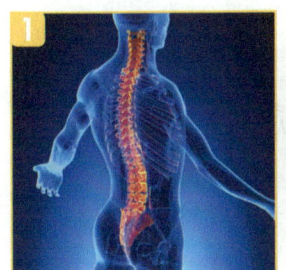

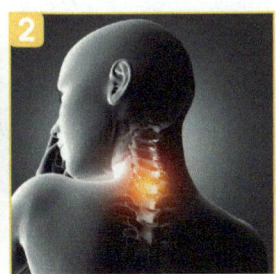

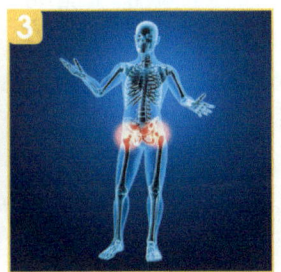

289

2. 朗读短语。Read the phrases aloud.

- 多人搬运
- 四人搬运
- 三人搬运
- 托住胸背部
- 托住臀部
- 托住下肢
- 颈椎损伤者
- 胸、腰椎损伤者
- 医护工作者

学习课文　Text　🎧 30-2

Duō rén bānyùn
多人搬运

Bānyùn jǐzhù sǔnshāng de shāngyuán, yídìng yào bǎochí shāngyuán jǐzhù shēnzhí.
搬运脊柱损伤的伤员，一定要保持伤员脊柱伸直。

Jǐngzhuī sǔnshāng zhě xūyào sì rén bānyùn. Yì rén gùdìng tóubù; sān rén dūn zài shāngyuán tóng cè, tuōzhù shāngyuán de xiōng bèibù、túnbù hé xiàzhī. Hǎn kǒulìng （yī èr sān）, sì rén yìqǐ bǎ shāngyuán fàng zài yìngzhì dānjià shàng. Xiōng、yāozhuī sǔnshāng zhě xūyào sān rén bānyùn, gēn bānyùn jǐngzhuī sǔnshāng shāngyuán yíyàng, dàn búyòng gùdìng tóubù.

颈椎损伤者需要四人搬运。一人固定头部；三人蹲在伤员同侧，托住伤员的胸背部、臀部和下肢。喊口令（1——2——3），四人一起把伤员放在硬质担架上。胸、腰椎损伤者需要三人搬运，跟搬运颈椎损伤伤员一样，但不用固定头部。

Multi-people Handling

When transporting patients with spinal injuries, it is important to keep the spine straight.

For patients with cervical vertebra injuries, four people to transporting. One person fixed their head; Three people squat on the same side of the injured person supporting the chest, back, buttocks, and lower limbs. Shout the command "one—two—three", all four put the patient together onto a hard stretcher.

For patients with chest or lumbar vertebra injuries need to be three people are needed, just like those with cervical spine injuries, but without the need to stabilize the head.

课文练习 Text Exercises

1. 判断正误。True or false.

1. 搬运脊柱损伤的病人，要保持病人的脊柱伸直。
2. 颈椎损伤者需要三人搬运。
3. 胸、腰椎损伤者需要四人搬运。
4. 搬运颈椎损伤者，要把伤员放在硬质担架上。

2. 选词填空。Fill in the blanks with the correct words.

1. 搬运脊柱损伤的病人，要一直保持脊柱_____。
   A 伸直　　　　B 固定　　　　C 抬高

❷ 一人固定头部，三人蹲在伤员_____侧。

　A 一样　　　　B 同　　　　　C 另

❸ 四人一起把伤员放在_____担架上。

　A 硬质　　　　B 软　　　　　C 轻

❹ 胸、腰椎损伤者需要三人搬运，但_____固定头部。

　A 需要　　　　B 保持　　　　C 不用

学习语法 Grammar

语法点 1　Grammar Point 1

副词：一定　Adverb: 一定

"一定"放在动词前面，加强坚决、确定的语气。否定形式是"一定不＋动词"。"不一定"表示不太确定的语气。

The adverb "一定" is used before the verb to strengthen the resolute and definite tone. The negative form is "一定＋不＋verb". "不一定" indicates an uncertain tone.

例句：

❶ Bānyùn jǐzhù sǔnshāng de shāngyuán, yídìng yào bǎochí shāngyuán jǐzhù shēnzhí.
搬运脊柱损伤的伤员，一定要保持伤员脊柱伸直。
When transporting patients with spinal injuries, it is important to keep the spine straight.

❷ Nǐ de bìng yídìng huì hǎo de.
你的病一定会好的。You will definitely recover from your illness.

❸ Nǐ yídìng yào zhùyì xiūxi.
你一定要注意休息。Make sure to get enough rest.

第 30 课 | 多人搬运

语法练习 1 Grammar Exercise 1

把"一定"放在句中合适的位置。Put "一定" in the right place in the sentence.

1. ＿＿搬运时，＿＿要保持＿＿伤员脊柱＿＿伸直。
2. ＿＿颈椎损伤的伤员＿＿要放在硬质＿＿担架上＿＿。
3. 病人＿＿要＿＿注意＿＿休息＿＿。
4. 护士＿＿要＿＿记住（jìzhù, remember）：时间＿＿就是＿＿生命。

语法点 2 Grammar Point 2

连词：但 The conjunction: 但

连词"但"用在第二个分句的开头，表示语义的转折，常与"虽然"搭配使用。
The conjunction "但" is used at the beginning of the second clause to indicate a semantic transition and is often used with "虽然".

例句：

1. Bānyùn yāozhuī sǔnshāng zhě de fāngfǎ gēn bānyùn jǐngzhuī sǔnshāng shāngyuán yíyàng, dàn búyòng gùdìng tóubù.
搬运腰椎损伤者的方法跟搬运颈椎损伤伤员一样，但不用固定头部。The method of transporting a patient with a lumbar vertebra injury is the same as transporting a person with a cervical vertebra injury, but without the need to stabilize the head.

2. Zhǐyāfǎ kěyǐ kuàisù zhǐxiě, dàn zhǐ shì jǐnjí cuòshī, xiàoguǒ bú tài hǎo.
指压法可以快速止血，但只是紧急措施，效果不太好。Finger-pressing manipulation can quickly stop bleeding, but it is only an emergency measure and it doesn't work very well.

3. Wǒ chīguò zhè zhǒng yào, dàn méiyǒu xiàoguǒ.
我吃过这种药，但没有效果。I have taken this medicine before, but it has no effect.

语法练习 2　Grammar Exercise 2

用"但"完成句子。Complete the sentences with "但".

1. 我吃过这种药　　没有效果

___

2. 搬运腰椎损伤者的方法也是这样　　不用固定头部

___

3. 用中文学习护理很难　　我要坚持（jiānchí, insist）

___

4. 我没学（xué, learn）过护理　　我很喜欢（xǐhuan, like）

___

汉字书写　Writing Chinese Characters

shì 式 式 式 式 式 式
式　式　式　式　式

chéng 成 成 成 成 成 成
成　成　成　成　成

huò 或 或 或 或 或 或 或
或　或　或　或　或

wǒ 我 我 我 我 我 我
我　我　我　我　我

职业拓展 Career Insight

The First Modern Medical College in China

The first modern medical college in China was Beijing Union Medical College (PUMC), which has a history of over 100 years. It is located near Wangfujing Street in the center of Beijing. Since its establishment, it has trained many influential doctors in the Chinese medical and pharmaceutical industries, playing a crucial role in the development of modern medicine in China. Its affiliated hospital, Peking Union Medical College Hospital (PUMCH), is renowned for its advanced medical technology, scientific research achievements, and innovation. It is considered one of the top public hospitals in China and is recognized internationally.

小结 Summary

词语 Words

朗读词语。Read the words aloud.

伸直	颈椎	腰椎
臀部	蹲	托住

语法 Grammar

朗读句子。Read the sentences aloud.

1. 搬运脊柱损伤的伤员，一定要保持伤员脊柱伸直。
2. 一定要把颈椎损伤者放在硬质担架上。
3. 胸、腰椎损伤者搬运跟搬运颈椎损伤伤员一样，但不用固定头部。
4. 病人吃过这种药，但没有效果。

课文理解 Text Comprehension

根据课文内容回答问题。Answer the questions according to the text.

1. 搬运脊柱损伤的伤员，一定要注意什么？

2. 颈椎损伤者需要几个人搬运？

3. 搬运颈椎损伤者时，蹲在伤员同侧的三个人分别做什么？

4. 搬运胸、腰椎损伤者跟搬运颈椎损伤者一样吗？

郑重声明

高等教育出版社依法对本书享有专有出版权。任何未经许可的复制、销售行为均违反《中华人民共和国著作权法》，其行为人将承担相应的民事责任和行政责任；构成犯罪的，将被依法追究刑事责任。为了维护市场秩序，保护读者的合法权益，避免读者误用盗版书造成不良后果，我社将配合行政执法部门和司法机关对违法犯罪的单位和个人进行严厉打击。社会各界人士如发现上述侵权行为，希望及时举报，我社将奖励举报有功人员。

反盗版举报电话　（010）58581999　58582371
反盗版举报邮箱　dd@hep.com.cn
通信地址　北京市西城区德外大街4号　高等教育出版社知识产权与法律事务部
邮政编码　100120

读者意见反馈

为收集对教材的意见建议，进一步完善教材编写并做好服务工作，读者可将对本教材的意见建议通过如下渠道反馈至我社。

咨询电话　0086-10-58581350
反馈邮箱　xp@hep.com.cn
通信地址　北京市西城区德外大街4号
　　　　　高等教育出版社海外出版事业部（国际语言文化出版中心）
邮政编码　100120